WICCA
FOR BEGINNERS

A STARTER KIT TO THE SOLITARY PRACTITIONER. GUIDE TO STARTING PRACTICAL MAGIC, BELIEF, SPELLS, MAGIC, SHADOW AND WITCHCRAFT RITUALS.

AMY LISA KRYSTAL

Wicca For Beginners:

A Starter Kit To The Solitary Practitioner. Guide To Starting Practical Magic, Belief, Spells, Magic, Shadow, And Witchcraft Rituals

Author Name

Amy Lisa Krystal

© Copyright 2019 – Amy Lisa Crystal –
All rights reserved.

The content contained within this book may not be reproduced, duplicated or transmitted without direct written permission from the author or the publisher.
Under no circumstances will any blame or legal responsibility be held against the publisher, or author, for any damages, reparation, or monetary loss due to the information contained within this book. Either directly or indirectly.

Legal Notice:
This book is copyright protected. This book is only for personal use. You cannot amend, distribute, sell, use, quote or paraphrase any part, or the content within this book, without the consent of the author or publisher.

Disclaimer Notice:
Please note the information contained within this document is for educational and entertainment purposes only. All effort has been executed to present accurate, up to date, and reliable, complete information. No warranties of any kind are declared or implied. Readers acknowledge that the author is not engaging in the rendering of legal, financial, medical or professional advice. The content within this book has been derived from various sources. Please consult a licensed professional before attempting any techniques outlined in this book.
By reading this document, the reader agrees that under no circumstances is the author responsible for any losses, direct or indirect, which are incurred as a result of the use of information contained within this

document, including, but not limited to, — errors, omissions, or inaccuracies.

Table of Contents

Introduction

Chapter 1 – Understand The History Of Wicca   8

THE BURNING TIME	12
THE RESURGENCE OF THE OLD RELIGION	14
HOW TO TREAT WITH THOSE OF ANOTHER RELIGION	15
CELTAS-PRE-WICCAS DRUIDS	17
Regarding Witchcraft	19
The Truth About Sorcerers	69
The Creation Of The Myths In Wicca	90
The Gods	91
THE EXISTENCE PLANS	93
THE ASTRAL PLANE	94
THE ELEMENTARY PLANE	97
THE HIDDEN DIMENSIONS	102
THE WICCA CODE	106
WHAT IS FORBIDDEN?	107
WHAT IS ALLOWED?	107
WHAT IS RECOMMENDED TO DO?	108
THE WICCAN LAWS	108
Statement Of Purpose	113
Membership Qualification	114
Degrees Of Participation And Membership	114

Membership Status _____ 117
The Coven Council _____ 117
THE WICCA SABBATS _____ **122**

Chapter 2 – The Link Between Wicca And Witchcraft 123

Chapter 3 – Learning Wiccan Spells _____ 133

Ceremonial Magic _____ 134
Herbs _____ 136

Chapter 4 - Wicca Terminologies _____ 138

Conclusion _____ 149

Introduction

Congratulations on purchasing *Wicca For Beginners* and thank you for doing so.

There are plenty of books on this subject on the market, thanks again for choosing this one! Every effort was made to ensure it is full of as much useful information as possible, please enjoy!

Its night the curtains of home High-class ones are tight to avoid prying eyes. Candles shine in the living room. The incense smoke twists in spirals. Figures in tunics are singing in a language. Water long forgotten, circulate around a table of rustic wood. Above her, among the candles, images Sacred: A Powerful Goddess, Using a Crescent Moon on the forehead; a God holding a spear in his raised hand.

All movements cease. A woman next to Altar says:
In this sacred space and time
We now call the Ancestors:
The Goddess of the Moon, the seas and the rivers;
The God of the radiated Sun, the valleys and the forests:
Approach us in this circle.

This is Witchcraft.

Two thousand miles away, a girl of fifteen Place a green candle over a friend's photo. At the Darkroom, she lights the candle. Then close your eyes. In her mind, she envisions a bright lilac light enveloping *in this space and sacred space and time* we now call the Ancestors Ancestors:
The Goddess of the Moon, the seas and the rivers;

The God of the radiated sun,
Sun, valleys, and forests:
Approach us in this circle.

Seeing her boyfriend's broken arm, she sings a healing magic wax. This is also Witchcraft. These two examples summarize Witchcraft. Popular wizards are people who are dissatisfied with beliefs based on religion or physics; they have landed the earth and its treasures. They turned to themselves to understand the mystical powers of the human body brother and to feel their connection to Earth and they found that magic works.

Chapter 1 – Understand The History Of Wicca

The first indications of the old Witchcraft / Religion date back 25,000 years BC. Dr. Margaret Murray did a study and traced the origins of the ancient religion. She saw an unbroken chain from that era to the present day of a religious system spread throughout Eastern Europe, many centuries before the appearance of Christianity. She presented evidence and theories about the origin of this religion, which to date are much respected. In the

Paleolithic era, men and women depended on hunting for survival. Only if the hunt was good would they have food, skins to cover themselves and bones to manufacture weapons and tools. Nature amazed them in such a way that in their amazement and fear of it attributed controlling spirits of those forces, turning them into deities. It is what we would call "Animism" today. As there was a god for every force of nature, there was also a god for hunting. Most of the animals that were hunted had horns, so men gave the appearance of man with horns to the god of the hunt. It is here where the magic is mixed for the first time with this model of worship to the gods.

The first manifestations of magic were sympathetic, that is, they believed that if they did an image of a biscuit molded in the mud, and then "killed", after hunting they would kill a real bison. The religious - magical rituals had been born that way, with one of the men dressed in skins and horns, representing the god, directed the "hunt" of the clay drum. Today there are still paintings in caves that date to that era and represent that ritual. Next to this god of hunting, there was a goddess. This was not about hunting, but about fertility, since if there were animals to kill, it was necessary that these same animals should reproduce to ensure the existence of animals to hunt. It is not known who emerged first, if the god or the goddess, and it is something that does not really matter, nor there is material to clarify it.

If the tribe were to be perpetuated, the fertility of its members was somewhat important for them, even more considering the high degree of morality that they had in those days. For sympathetic magic, animal figures copulating are molded in the mud, and accompanied in the ritual members of the clan. There are many images of the Goddess that were found in excavations, in which they reflect the importance they gave to the genital aspect of women, symbolizing their fertility and sexuality. These have large breasts, swollen belly, and exaggerated sexual organs, leaving aside aspects such as arms, legs and face. With the development of agriculture, the need for hunting declined, and that caused arise of the goddess. She now also began to take care of the fertility of the earth, as well as the tribe and the animals. In this way the year was divided into two halves.

The summer in which food grew from the earth was dominated by the Goddess, and the winter in which food was obtained through hunting, was dominated by God. The other deities (thunder, wind, rain, etc.) became secondary gods then in aspects of the god and the goddess. As man evolved, so did religion, to what it is today. Men scattered throughout Europe, taking with them their gods. When the new countries were created, the gods acquired new names, although not so different, however being the same gods. When the man learned to store his crops in barns for winter, hunting became even less necessary, so the God of the hunt became the God of the nature, death and beyond.

THE BURNING TIME

It is known as a fiery era, one in which all who did not believe or embrace the catholic religion, were burned alive or hanged (in some countries it was not allowed burn nobody, so they hung them up). It is interesting to note that at this time many of the people who died, not even they were wiccans, but only people who were not loved in their villages and therefore were accused as witches. It is no less interesting to notice how the ignorance of Christianity accused the sorcerers of being devil worshipers and to kill children, when in reality there is no such practice among the wiccans since we don't believe in the devil since that goes against the burden of the Goddess and against love and respect for everything living. It is estimated that the total number of executions (according to the Catholic Church) was 3,000. The severity of the persecution was not uniform throughout Europe; concentrated first in eastern France, Germany and Switzerland. Many countries got rid of burning. The burning era and its persecution greatly diminished with the Arrival of the Age of Enlightenment, when people started asking about religious "truths" held for a long time.

This forced the end of the Execution of sorcerers in Europe and America. The important thing of that time for us, more than the numbers of how many died, is that the laws of inquisition were abolished. Today we are still victims of persecution for the fact that our beliefs are different from those of others religions and although they do not burn us alive or take us to the gallows, it is something with which we must live daily, especially those who live in countries with high Christian morality.

THE RESURGENCE OF THE OLD RELIGION

In 1951, in England, the last laws against sorcerers were abolished. In 1954, Gerald Gardner, published a book called "Witchcraft Today" in which he claims that

Murray's theories were correct and confessed to being sure of it since he himself was a Warlock. He also argued that possibly the Old Religion was about to disappear, but his surprise was that when the book circulated, he began to have news of Groups or Covens scattered throughout Europe. The Old Religion has come a long way since its humble origins in the Prehistory to the present day. It has grown greatly and today is a religion known worldwide, thanks to all those who in one way or another decided to embrace the faith and make it public. To this we must add that thanks to the Internet, many more people are getting to know Wicca and being interested in this philosophy of life, which unlike other religions, they urge man to realize himself in a complete, free and therefore happy.

HOW TO TREAT WITH THOSE OF ANOTHER RELIGION

There is something we must always keep in mind, and that is when we meet before people who do not share our beliefs, the term "Warlock", bothers them of entrance and associate it directly with satanism. Therefore, I always recommend using the term "Wicca". Besides not knowing what it means, they are not so scared. Another thing we have to keep in mind is that, the burning era is over, and it doesn't have why there is enmity between Christianity and Wicca. Everyone should follow their way, and worry about studying their doctrines to stand firm in them throughout moment. We must study and know what our beliefs are based on so that when sharing with someone who doesn't know, let's be prepared to explain. What we believe and answer your questions. Another thing to consider is also whether we will be witches "OUT OF THE CLOSET" or inside of the closet ... that is, if we will say publicly that we are sorcerers, or we will keep it a secret; either way is fine. It is our choice, and many times we have to do what is best for us.

Today, there are many who may accuse us of being devil worshipers, of killing guys on "Halloween", or meet up to invoke spirits. If we know what we are and what we do, all these accusations will pass us by. So the best preparation to deal with those of other religions is to study; worry about what we believe and live a lifestyle accordingly. If we do, no one can tell us anything, and even more, they will resort to when we have problems, since we will be the "NEIGHBORHOOD WISES".

CELTAS-PRE-WICCAS DRUIDS

Around 250 BC, the Roman advance made him start the conquest of region gala, occupied by the Celts, whose beliefs little known they were quite distorted above all by Catholicism, which took some elements, such as the organization of his priestly class and the cult of Hesu, the son that his own sacrifice to save men; the manuscripts or compilations of the studies of the disciples of the Priestly colleges were copied and transmitted in secret or all Eastern and Central Europe, in part by merchants and collectors. The Gauls had a highly symbolic cult, their doctrine believed in the immortality of the soul and its cult was classified into categories, similar to those of medieval monks; their priests were legislators, doctors, poets and capable to get in touch with the spiritual world, they attribute power to the stars and influence on men and nature, knew and dominated the herbal therapy, his priests were infallible fortune tellers, consulted by noble and even by Emperor Aurelian. In many cultures they are also the last court to appeal to, rented guns, for those who ask for extraordinary help to get a partner or get revenge on someone. The English word "witch" (sorcerer), derives from the Anglo-Saxon Wicca (with the female form wicce), a word used today by many sorcerers as a synonym for the "Ancient Religion." It can relate to the words "wit" and "wise" (wit and wise) and with a term that means "folded", and that continues with words like "witch hazel". The word "wicked" suggests that in England the Witch connotations had a mainly negative sense. ("Warlock"(sorcerer), often used by later writers referring to a male and lonely sorcerer, is completely pejorative in its original meaning; refers to someone who alters or breaks an oath.) More neutral terms were "cunning man" and "cunning woman", employed in the English Renaissance to refer to the seers and healers of a town, who were engaged in what was considered "white magic." Words from other languages tend to show the same mixed feelings.

Regarding Witchcraft

The toughest is perhaps the Italian strega, coming from the Latin word that designates an ulcer, and that came to be applied to a vampire. The Greek Pharmakos identifies the sorcerer with the poison expert. But, in general, the words simply refer to the fact that the sorcerer is the one who makes use of witchcraft of one kind or another. The French sorcerer, the German hexel and zauberin, the Spanish sorcerer and the Russian vedyna, lack the horror felt by the people of Mediterranean towards the relatives of the dreaded

Circe, who, according to Homer, converted Ulysses sailors in pigs.

In English, the word "witch", like the Anglo-Saxon wicca, refers both to a man as a woman, but the repeated English distinction between "witchcraft" and "sorcey" (sorcery), does not occur in many languages. The word "witchcraft" has almost always been used in a negative sense, for historical reasons that denote the prejudices of medieval ecclesiastics, who condemned anything belonging to the world of magic, as a sign that the Devil instead of Christ. The wizards of the twentieth century have worked to rehabilitate that Wicca image, or "the Art of the Wise," seeking to ratiate himself with the church admitting that medieval witchcraft was actually religious exercise. My opinion is that this effort to separate sorcery witchcraft does more than obscure the constant interaction between a popular magic and the practices of a more intellectual occultism (the so-called high or ceremonial magic).The practices of contemporary witch meetings, for example, cannot be understood without referring to the ceremonial magic of the Renaissance, which revived in the19th century through groups such as the Golden Dawn.

On the other hand, the tradition of ceremonial magic, which we will talk about later, is full of popular practices, remains of older perspectives. What do we really know about the tradition of witchcraft in the West? What I made clear was that there were two separate legends and a composite story of facts. The first legend was developed during the centuries of persecution, which culminated in the almost incredible barbarism of the sixteenth and seventeenth centuries. The second is the legend of the "Old Religion" of the cult witches of the twentieth century. The history of the facts is a complex story, in which the Popular magic of ancient Europe mixed with the sunken waste Hellenic civilization, to form the basis of the first legend and practices and covert beliefs of today's hereditary sorcerers.

Since I started working backwards, starting from the second legend, in my effort to penetrate Tanya's world of magic, maybe that is the best point for us to start. In this book we will sketch the history of the "Ancient Religion," as told by folklorists of the nineteenth century, and have actually transformed modern sorcerers. It should be noted that Shakespeare's best works share the ingredients that they made La Semilla del Diablo a blockbuster: sex, violence ... and what hidden. The Elizabethan auditoriums, like the contemporaries, enjoyed the presentation of ghosts (Hamlet), witches (Macbeth) and supernatural beings (The dream of a summer night). After all, it was still a time when men and women could be judged for the damage resulting from the practice of black magic. Over time, the views of men like Scot and Hobbes became norm for an urban and educated population. However, in rural areas, the Old beliefs - and old fears - disappeared more slowly. Tanya remembers, for example, that the inhabitants of the beautiful Devonshire region, where he attended the school, accepted the presence of elementary spirits, fairies, in all things crescent surrounding them. Such rural practices and beliefs are not only characteristic of England, but from all over the West. Primitive folklorists, such as Jacobo Grimm, suggested association between these schemes and the paganism that the church had tried to exterminate in the Middle Ages.

Witchcraft, in particular, was considered a relic of the oldest European religions, especially the cult of Diana, goddess of the moon. At the end of the nineteenth century, the American journalist Charles Godfrey Leland, who wrote several volumes on the folklore of northern Italy believed he found conclusive evidence that the "Old Religion" had survived, even beyond the last of his appearances that he had news, three centuries before. With the help of a young strega, called Maddalena, he gathered a small and remarkable collection of material, which he titled Aradia, or the Gospel of the Sorcerers. It included a self-titled Vangelo or gospel, which narrated the birth of Aradia, the goddess of the witchcraft, instructions for a ritual meal in honor of Diana and Aradia, collection of spells and various legends attesting to the existence of Counter religion references to oppression that appear in Aradia suggest the same type of period turbulent that the Franciscans had produced and the heretical sect of the Waldensians (the Poor Men of Lyon), a 12th-century group that advocated a profound asceticism and great personal piety, in contrast to wealth and style basically formal institutional church.

The Waldensian influence remained strong in northern Italy, through the medieval and modern ages, and it is very possible that would contribute to the general mood of the Leland manuscript. But, apart from this, I doubt that the legend of Aradia had roots as old as Leland supposed. All the 19th century was a time of romantic reconstructions of the era of Greece and Rome, and the structural simplicity of the myth, so different from the confusing versions of most of the folk tales that have reached us through the centuries, the intervention suggests from the hand of someone who knew the classics, who had ease of poetic expression, as well as a fervent hatred for the church and for the aristocracy of landowners. Leland mentions his belief that witch covens (meeting rituals) continue to be celebrated, even within the Holy City. However, spells and narratives that he adds to his basic text suggest only the individualistic practices that generally characterize European popular magic.

There were sorcerer meetings in northern Italy? In a region where witchcraft was practiced with little fear of official reprisals, the absence of more explicit references to Group activities seem a clear enough indication that they were not held. That nostalgia, found in many of the occultists of the time, is the key to understand why seemingly mundane men dressed in exotic costumes; they pronounced enchantments in an impossible language and acted in general as if the future of humanity depended on something other than the expansion of industrial civilization. However, the reality is that the end of the nineteenth century witnessed the existence of many groups dedicated to the study and practice of magic. The Witchery, in the opinion of the adherents of the Hermetic Order of the Golden Dawn, in England, of the Order of the Temple of the East, in Germany, was an adulterated Christianity, a Worship of the Devil, who did not deserve the consideration of educated men. The Aradla de Leland, published in 1899, did not attract much attention and was soon forgotten. Margaret Murray, the lady who made witchcraft intellectually respectable, he never refers to her in his two main books, and neither is mentioned in the pages of The Witchcraft Today, by Gerald B. Gardner, which opened the contemporary round of revelations regarding the "Old Religion". Thomas C. Leffibridge, whose book Bruges again presented Leland's work to the modern pubic, he commented that "it seems weird and is likely to be drowned in some way for hidden interests. " A better explanation is likely that even the discovery of a sect dedicated to Diana in the distant Italy will not show that the groups dedicated to witchcraft of the Middle Ages, if they came into existence, they would have survived in the modern world. There is an interval of two centuries between Aradia and The Witchcraft Cult in Occidental Europe, by Margaret Murray. Upside down from Leland, Miss Murray did not pretend that organized witchcraft would have survived their persecutors. What he did offer was a remarkable and profound study in support of his thesis that witchcraft, while it existed, it was a different religion, which coexisted with Christianity during the Middle Ages. This theory does not demand a belief in the possibility of miraculous facts. Despite the title of his book, Murray largely limited his study to the British Islands. It began with a critical distinction between "operational witchcraft," or the various practices of folk magic, and "ritual witchcraft" or the forms of a rooted religion at a level of civilization that preceded the development of agriculture. His theory is that this religion, which she says has a god, in the form of a man or of a beast, well-defined rites and excellent organization, survived the Advent of the Christian church.

The great trials for witchcraft, which began in Brittany with the prosecution of Alice Kyteler, in 1324, they were a determined and finally fortunate effort to be part of Christian clerics to suppress their former rivals. But, just like Miss Murray rebuilds, those prosecutions did not have only one religious character, but also included the struggle for political power among peoples originating in Europe and its successors oriented by Rome.

What differentiated Margaret Murray's study from previous works on witchcraft was his total acceptance of the material provided by the "confessions" of the tortured by sorcerers. The writers that preceded them took them for their nominal value, as proof of a perverted Christianity, or rejected them entirely, as the product of the imagination of the clergy. In The Witchcraft Cult in the Western Europe are considered statements about facts about what Murray called the "Diánico cult". The devil - or god - of sorcerers, who was said they worshiped in ritual meetings, he was a man dressed in black, to hide his true identity, or covered with animal skin to represent the divinity of nature (the Cuckold God) that was the object of worship. The thirteen groups members (twelve worshipers and the one who was dressed as God) were destined organizations to worship. Ten years after the publication of her first book, Margaret Murray wrote The God of the Sorcerers. By then I had already fully accepted the idea that Fairies of legend were the Pygmy aboriginal inhabitants of Western Europe.

They were also the heirs of the "Old Religion", and the conquerors, who wanted to count on their loyalty, they learned to adopt their customs. For that reason they were adept at the Diánico cult among the most members relevant of the royal courts of England and France. Murray had already presented his thesis that both Joan of Arc and the remarkable Gillesde Rais, executed in 1440 by mass murderer, had been heads of associations of sorcerers. In a second book he added the names of William Rufus, the English king killed in New Forest in 1100, and Thomas Becket, as people who professed the "Old Religion." He said of the four that had been the human sacrifices required at the end of each seven-year cycle of the reign of a king.

According to this theory, William Rufus died by himself, but the other three, ironically, two were canonized by the church they opposed, were ritual substitutes Juana and Gilles de Rais died instead of Carlos VIII, and Becket. He died for Henry II. This extraordinary statement implied that not only the kings of France and England but also high members of the Catholic hierarchy, such as the saint Archbishop Thomas Becket, they were only nominally Christians. It also meant that the idea of a divine victim was basic to the understanding of medieval politics. As could be expected, this theory made Margaret Murray lose much of her reputation as a serious historian. But she, undaunted, published in 1954, the year of The Witchcraft Today of Gerald B. Gardner, The Divine King in England, an affirmation end of his conviction that British royalty had accepted the "Old Religion", from Roman times to the seventeenth century.

Margaret Murray's books have become a kind of gospel for the contemporary sorcerers, like the Aradia de Leland. More than anything else, they created the legend of the "Old Religion", continued by Gerald Gardner, Sybil Leek, Alex Sanders, Raymond Buckland

and the many others who have claimed to be current worshipers of the Cuckold God and the moon goddess. Nothing is known about to what extent Miss Murray influenced not only the legitimization of associations of groups that surfaced after World War II, but also where they were possible. There is no certain test that such associations existed in England before the appearance, in1921, from The Cult of Witchcraft in Western Europe.

At the beginning of the eighteenth century, English law, reacting so much because of the tragic experiences of the colonial magistrates of Salem, as per the new climate of rationalism, reversed the position he had held throughout its history. No longer would people be persecuted for witchcraft. Now those claims would be precisely the outlaws. But this new law did not come into force until 1951, retained mainly because of the lobbying of the spiritualists and not because nobody believed that there were sorcerers to practice freely your knowledge without fear of punishment. But in 1954, Gerald B. Gardner, former plantation owner and officer of customs in Malaysia, who had retired to New Forest, in England, published The Witchcraft Today as an affirmation that there were ritual meetings of sorcerers and the time had come for details of that science to be made public. In his book, for which Margaret Murray wrote an introduction, he repeated the story of the "Little Town", presented in The God of Sorcerers.

In Gardner's opinion, the Neolithic cult schemes, specifically the cult of God Cuckold, came to suffer the influence of the cult of the Great Mother, when a Celtic population to the aboriginal pygmies of Western Europe. That Druid cult tended, in turn, to adopt the colors of the successive waves of invaders, until in the Middle Ages. Contrary to the theory of Margaret Murray, most of the Warlocks considered themselves good Christians. But the Knowledge had survived, even through the time of persecution. Gardner's introduction to Knowledge is a fascinating story. Gardner discovered that some of his neighbors in the New Forest region were members of hidden group founded by the daughter of the theosophist Annie Besant. It was the Congregation of Crotone, named after the esoteric group founded by Pythagoras in the former Italy. Some of the members of the congregation finally confessed to Gardner who had established contact with the last members of an ancient ritual group.

Gardner, meanwhile, met the old woman who had led the group and was initiated by her to witchcraft. After the woman's death, Gardner wrote a novel, The Help of High Magic, in which he revealed the uninterrupted existence of the tradition of ritual associations. That was in 1949, two years before witchcraft Stopped being illegal. In 1954 he published The Witchcraft Today, raising the curtain of mystery that covered up the activities of his own group. Gardner, who had previously been a student of Malaysian magic, was working on a new reputation with the study of witchcraft. In addition to supervising a multitude of new Ritual groups, he opened a Museum of Magic and Witchcraft on the Isle of Man, a place whose inhabitants possessed, according to Gardner, all the characteristics of the "Little Town". Gardner claimed that he was transmitting the Knowledge, and not rebuilding it. But Sybil Leek does not accept that the nudity and ritual sex that characterized the meetings (and also the dissident groups associated with Alex Sanders) are authentic. Francis King, one of the contemporary writers on the more trained modern occult, suggests that Gardner was limited to giving free rein to his exhibitionist and sadomasochistic tendencies with the rites he proposed, adding that at the beginning of the 1940s he commissioned the not very well reputed Aleister Crowley to prepare four of the rites to be used in a cult of the resurrected witchcraft.

The late fifties and early sixties were the height of the new ritual groups, even though the enormous publicity that would allow the "Old Religion" will be fragmented into a hundred heresies. Sybil Leek was appointed high priestess of an association close to Nice, which had been governed until then by an old Russian aunt of his. He then returned to New Forest, where he had an antique shop, to give rise to the ritual group Horsa. Alex Sanders, who had started his study of witchcraft with his Welsh grandmother, and then made some incursions by black magic before joining one of the new groups. Gerald Gardner died in 1964. The man who continued Gardner's work, particularly in the United States, was Raymond Buckland. He was a writer as well as editor of old works, such as the Aradia de Leland, he began his own version of a witchcraft museum in Long Island. In

1969, a year after Sybil Leek's Diary of A Witch, June Johns wrote The King of Warlocks: The World of Alex Sanders. One of those converted by that description of Sanders's concept of the term wicca was Stewart Farrar, a journalist published in 1971. What the Sorcerers Do: The Modern Nude Ritual group, book in which he narrated his own quick initiation to knowledge and a complete description of one of the "Alexandrian" rituals.

What is left to tell? Francis King, who shares my suspicion that modern groups of sorcerers did not come alive until after the publication of Margaret Murray's first book, accepts that there were two English groups when Gardner arrived in New Forest. It is possible that they came to determine how they were influenced by the content of the Book of Shadows, one of the various manuscripts in which the high Priestess of a ritual group must record the rites celebrated by her group. I have seen two printed versions of the Book of Shadows. One is quite a vulgar set of enchantments equivalent to the manuscript of an occultist. The other is the copy written by the "Queen of the Witches of America," Lady Sheba, and presented by Llewellyn Publications. Lady Sheba's manual is divided into three parts: laws, rituals and covens. Indications are included in the text of the laws about the behavior of a witch if she is tortured. If authentic, they would show that Wicca laws date back at least at the beginning of the seventeenth century.

The rites follow the standard pattern of the vast majority of ritual groups. The Wizards perform their naked rites, within a circle of nine feet in diameter, traced by the high priestess with a consecrated knife (athame). Inside the circle is an altar with everything you need (candles, water, salt, a bell, a whip of rope) for the rites. There are eight Great Coven (Sabbats), or important festivals (for example, the eve of All Saints) and twenty-six Esbats, coinciding with the New and full moons, and each one must be celebrated with the appropriate symbolism. In the festivals in which sorcerers should be initiated to any of the three degrees of Knowledge, there are additional rites that require, among other things, "the five-fold kiss" (on the feet, knees, groin, chest and lips), a soft flogging and convenient admonitions. Apart from nudity and flogging, they don't have necessarily erotic tone in the most serious ritual groups. There are few things in Lady

Sheba's text that can annoy a normal person. Of course, there is nothing about harm to another person, typical of the stereotyped version sorcerer. Taken at face value, Modern group rituals that he describes are poetic and kind evocations of the rhythm of nature. The Devil is noted for his absence. Since any version of the Book of Shadows is necessarily a product of a living tradition is impossible, as I have already pointed out, to say to what extent it is relatively recent work of Lady Sheba and how much of him is prior to Gerald Gardner. Tanya tells me that her grandmother's "Black Book" was known as the "Book of Calls" and contained several demonic invocations, written in what seemed to be a Latin upside down. This suggests that the originals of what is now known as Book of Shadows were nothing but magic books or black magic manuals that were used since the Middle Ages, to which they had gone adding scraps of an oral tradition related to the procedures of ritual groups.

This oral tradition could begin when a lone sorcerer passed his knowledge to another; group rules may have been developed gradually, by taking for granted those sorcerers who were ideally supposed to meet in groups.

But there may never be a way to know with sure what the true story of these modern groups is, and what is not. No discussion about contemporary witchcraft is complete without reference to purported Satanism of Anton LaVey, who considers all traditional religions fraudulent and psychologically destructive. Ancient occultist, who had professions as varied as lion tamer and police photographer, LaVey converted in 1966 a group that met to discuss occultism in the First Church of Satan. His house in San Francisco became the center where they celebrated Black Masses, to which great publicity was given, and in which they were all necessary attachments: a naked woman as an altar, theatrical invocations to the devil and the advice of practicing the "seven deadly sins." LaVey, whose sense of theatricality exceeds even Alex Sanders, has shown to be a master of occult fantasy, in the purest style of Aleister Crowley. The Satanic Bible, one of the various books he has written, expresses a consistent philosophy in which the Devil appears as the symbol of all human desires repressed by orthodox Christianity.

The Devil cult in the Satanic Church tries to satisfy a human need for rites, while allowing an expression therapy of sensuality and hostilities that are part of the human condition. LaVey's conception of witchcraft as a set of techniques to focus on latent paranormal capabilities it may not be anything other than one day up to date of the renewed "Magick" of Aleister Crowley, but has not stopped to irritate other cult wizards.

The question of whether witchcraft should be considered a religion was raised shortly after Tanya's dear grandmother's death from cancer. This one had begun to have repeated sleep, which gave great emphasis to a feeling of loss, which is the central point to most of the theological conceptions of hell. In the dream, the Loss was caused by their refusal to adopt any religious beliefs. According to your psychiatrist, who had come sporadically since childhood, for reasons of therapy, the dream meant that Tanya had not yet faced the specifically religious dimension of human mortality. Surprised and saddened by the death of his grandmother, he could not find any meaning. The doctor asked how it was possible for Tanya to say that she was a witch and will not identify with some kind of religious experience. She insisted on her atheism and the psychiatrist pointed out with identical resolution the evidence of religious concern that sprouted from his subconscious. Finally, he had to admit that he believed in God and that the perspective of his magic acquired a new quality because of this belief.

It is difficult, if not impossible, to draw a line between the spheres of magic and religion. Both refer to the world in terms that go beyond the narrow limits of what today we consider a nascent awareness, the distinction between discovery of transcendence to which man responds with worship and the recognition of a harmony, with which you try to synchronize through its symbols. From this perspective, it is understandable that magic should continually employ religious framework for their practices and that religion should be enhanced by adopting the robes of magic. Tanya, who has finally discovered a certain religious feeling, shares in this aspect the position of the cult witches, who since the days of Gerald Gardner have proclaimed that their rites have an intrinsically religious perspective. It's possible that the one that has gone further in this direction has been Sybil Leek; in The Artful of Witchcraft comes to develop a theology for the "Ancient Religion," mixing Asian concepts about the duality of nature (such as in the Chinese concepts of Ying and Yang), karma and the theme of lunar worship, with which already Aradia familiarized us.

This religious zeal indicates the extent to which the ritual groups today they are the natural heirs of the moralizing secret societies of an era previous. Is it a religious experience compatible with the most familiar tradition Judeo-Christian? Anton LaVey scoffed at those who accepted the "Old Religion", for lacking the courage to see themselves as authentic anti-Christians, but their own opinions are supported by a fairly partial presentation of Christianity. According to Gerald Gardner there was no problem that a person was a Christian, although heterodox, and witch, and I don't know of any ritual group of their tradition that demands the explicit renunciation of Christianity that was part of the medieval legend. These concepts may upset many fundamentalist Christians somewhat, but it is a widespread point of view among sorcerers themselves. Earlier, I had said that young people who have accepted the idea of witchcraft as part of the counterculture generally have not given any religious practices.

Many are willing to follow Anton LaVey and Philips Bonewits (author of Real Magic) in its totally materialistic conception of magic. But in my opinion, that has not prevented the return of magic from being a religious phenomenon. Witchcraft may not always be a complete belief system in itself, but it is something that works in the absence of other beliefs to satisfy specifically religious need, the need to find meaning in the person who transcends the limits of ordinary experience and gets a kind of experience in which the reality of this transcendence is confirmed. Religious needs are not equally strong in all people or in all cultural environments. They occur in their most amazing ways when others falter institutional forces. The first ritual groups of the 1950s coincided with a theatrical increase in the attractiveness of the church, after the chaos of the Second World War and Cold War tensions. In both periods, men watched inward and religion and magic gained numerous adherents at the same time.

Occultism disguised as counterculture, born of the reaction against Vietnam, had great acceptance in the public imagination, at the same time that it began to charge it forms a strong and new fundamentalism, with which they called themselves the People of Jesus. As a historian I have to point out that the legend of the "Old Religion", although has been beautifully presented, remains a very recent addition to the central flow of western occultism. However, and for the most serious wizards, Wicca satisfies a real need, and they alone compete to judge the validity of the religious experience that they extract from it. Today Tanya can say of herself that she is a witch, but three centuries ago a similar statement in the Christian world would have provided an invitation to appear before local magistrates, which could involve torture and even death to have committed the most horrific crime that the medieval mind could conceive.

Of course, this has not always been the case, not everywhere. In Russia, for example, there have never been such enormous persecutions of the witchcraft that characterized Western Europe. Tanya's grandmother once told us how they had killed almost all the people of her village, in a pogrom that occurred when she was a very small girl. It was not necessary to look for those who trafficked with the Devil, when the Jews were at hand to absorb the aggressions caused by a hostile environment and undocumented. And remembering the horror of my parenting period, Europe showed itself well prepared to resort to the pogrom again, when it became necessary to seek victims for the dark gods of material success.

The fact that Tanya is a witch and a Jew is a simple coincidence. The irony is that yes we would still live under medieval laws, Tanya would probably be acquitted of the accusation of witchcraft because she is not a baptized Christian and cannot, therefore, be apostate, as every witch is supposed to be by definition. However, given their knowledge of the world of magic, both in beliefs and practices, he would condemn the laws that forbade witchcraft, and could still be asked, under torture, everything he knew about the renegade Christians who went to the "covens" and the "synagogues" of sorcerers. In some regions, although they left it amusingly open, because it is his first crime, could be forced to wear a head dress, known as "bean hat", as a sign of his public misfortune.

Although modern treatises on witchcraft find romantic term origins "sabbat" (coven), which differentiates it from the Jew "sabbath" (Jewish Saturday), until a superficial knowledge of medieval sources indicates that a crude anti-Semitism imposed this custom. For example, witch clusters are frequently called "synagogues"; the term "coven" does not appear in the literature of the trials, until being used in Scotland at the end of the seventeenth century. The head of the witch rides, in the regions and periods in which this concept was fundamental in the image of a witch, ritual meeting of thirteen sorcerers. Frequently other than Herodias, the scandalous queen who got her daughter asks the head of John the Baptist in a tray. In the worst periods of witchcraft panic of the sixteenth and seventeenth centuries, sorcerers were frequently accused of the same antisocial activities (poisoning, murder of children) that were previously attributed to the Jews. And finally, like the Jews, the sorcerer is not condemned for what he does but for what he is ... he who has turned against Christ.

The implicit association of Judaism with witchcraft is, in my opinion, the key to the understanding of the medieval legend of the witch, which finally led to fantasies like Aradia and the Celtic reconstructions of

Margaret Murray and Gerald Gardner. It also explains why in a country like Spain there were few persecutions and there was no hysteria, while Western Europe was convulsing in its entirety in fear of sorcerers.

The Spanish church was too busy with the Moors, the Jews and the Muslims, who had converted only nominally to Catholicism, after edict of Fernando and Isabel by which the exile of non-Christians was demanded. In Italy, another country in which the madness of the sorcerers did not explode, it was enough with the fear of Protestants. Although the real story is much more complicated than the legend of the "Antigua Religion" explained by Margaret Murray, there is some truth in her statement that the Witchcraft tradition implied a pagan backdrop. At the beginning of time, there were two social classes capable of resisting forced Christianization. It was the people of the country (the pagans, according to the Latin word that designates a country region) that, like the Indian and mestizo populations of Latin America today, turned Catholicism into a disguise of older practices. The other was the instructed aristocracy. Many non-Christian aristocrats, men of fortune and culture, resisted until the 6th century, two hundred years after Constantine, generally admitting as chaplains from his house to the deposed professors of Greek philosophy, who had already been integrated with the remains of the Greek religion in the early Christian era, and sending their children to be educated in philosophy schools. When the Muslim invaders ended what had remained of the Roman Empire in the south and east, they found that traditions of magic alchemy, astrology and sorcery were still alive, despite the persistent efforts of Christianity to suppress them.

It should be noted that the highly Intellectualized Hellenistic magic could reach Western Europe again thanks to Islam. Two problems occurred in the population of remote rural regions. There was always resistance caused by the continuation of old practices, and the danger of a relapse in heretical beliefs was partially palliated by the church taking over the festivities, "baptizing" local divinities ("San" Cristóbal or "San" Jorge) and adopting old customs (decorating a fir tree for Christmas or decorating eggs for Easter). The orgiastic fertility rites were not assimilated so easily and in the old literature read cases of pastors who received a reprimand for having encouraged such holidays.

The other problem, which proved to be the most difficult, was the appeal of the heretics or visionaries for a people that was already beginning to resent power and privileges of the Catholic clergy. More formidable than reformers like the Waldensians, who they moved from Lyon to Italy, it was the dualistic orientation of Persian Zoroastrianism (the idea of good and evil, light and dark, spirit and matter, God and the Devil are realities other than a struggle for the soul of men), which prevailed in many of the groups that opposed the new Christian church. The Persian prophet Mani used this dualism to structure a church in the century, following the lines drawn by the Catholic hierarchy, and its philosophy (Manichaeism) was kept alive through a series of medieval movements, which they included.

The Dominican order was originally founded to combat the influence of the Cathars through more effective preaching, and the combative mood of those priests was one of the main factors in the persecution of witches, when the Cathars were annihilated. The country people, who were barely able to correctly retain the subtleties of Orthodox theology, could not avoid a certain distortion of heresy. A shout against the wealth of the church, for example, could become a 'bloody revolt against all who had taken power in the name of Christ'. In isolated areas of medieval Europe there were real devil worshipers and that was based on the legend of witchcraft, as developed later. The church itself was not in a position to appreciate the extent to which the survival of pagan forms and the influence of heresies like the Cathars ("the purified ones") had mixed to give rise to the belief in sorcerers.

Every act of sorcery, however trivial it was, had been regarded as diabolical by the most orthodox theologians, and the presence at the same time of popular magic and true diabolism in the same heralded to an understandable identification of the two. He also produced a paranoia ecclesiastical, which remained in force until when the usual reasons to fear Witchcraft, such as epidemics or devastating storms, did not occur. But this identification was not complete. The old attitude against paganism and new fear of heresy caused a curious contradiction even in their own Church documents. At a time when the church was very busy degrading the old practices, an ordinance appeared in the court of Charlemagne denouncing the popular belief that there were women riding in the skies following the hosts of the goddess Diana.

According to this Canon Episcopi, the priests had to explain that such a ride was an illusion created by the Devil to separate Christians from their faith in God, as the only source of miraculous power. By misinterpretation of the collection of decrees among which the Canon Episcopi appearedin the 10th century, it was understood that it came from the Council of Ancyra of the IV century and therefore he had the strength of a dogma. Reading it in its strict sense, it seemed to condemn one of the essential beliefs of so many later persecutors: the miraculous transport of sorcerers to the remote regions in which they celebrated their "covens". The unaffected defenders of the proposition that sorcerers actually performed those night flights insisted on the difference between the pagans mentioned by the Canon Episcopi and a new and more dangerous sect, a cult of sorcerers that had begun in the early fifteenth century.

The fact that theologians continued to discuss the details of witchcraft could be a factor that contributed to the decline of mass trials, at the end of the eighteenth century, but rarely helped those accused of witchcraft. The sorcerer was condemned for what he was, no for what he did. It was so sinful for the church to indulge in an orgy entirely imaginary how to attend such jaranas in person. If we did not forget that sorcery had been punishable even in pagan Rome, we will better understand how judgments that were accepted when it was about to expire the Roman Empire, over the course of several centuries could become legalized butcher shop of gigantic proportions, an avalanche that ended with the last doubts of personal freedom.

The tragic thing was that only when this had already happened did the public opinion and hysteria cease. How many died before that? Many writers accept the exaggerated figures of extremely jealous pursuers and talk about nine million deaths; the horrendous figure of two hundred thousand seems closer tithe truth. The legend of witchcraft, as an evil other than mere sorcery, began to charge momentum in the eighth century. In

1022, in the French city of Orleans, a trial was held by heresy in which the accusations of sexual orgies and cannibalism were cited, which the Romans already had employed against the Christians and the Christians against the Jews.

There was also talk of instant transport to obscene rituals, in which the Devil in the form of a black man would appear. In 1335, the Inquisition held in Toulouse and Carcassonne, former heretical centers, several notable judgments for two reasons. First, the use of the term "sabbat" to indicate specific days for worship; second, the application of torture for obtaining the necessary confessions, so that the suspects could be delivered by the church to the state, "the secular arm", for its execution. Half a century later, the proceedings and the charges of the trials were not as frequent as some wished. Actually, it almost always seemed that local representatives of the law did not appreciate the enormity of the diabolic conspiracy that existed since the advent of the fifteenth century and it was necessary to wake up an enthusiastic pursuer.

Apparently it was a rather ruthless man, who had made friends with very powerful people in Rome, and through them got in 1474 a papal appointment as inquisitor for southern Germany. In 1476, Institutoris were submerged in its witch-hunter's eagerness, but often found themselves with their hands tied by the procedural requirements that restricted the scope of the Inquisition. Ten years after his appointment, Institutoris obtained a document from the Pope Innocent VIII, for which he granted him and his inquisitor comrade, Jacob Sprenger full authority for the witch hunt, thus freeing his peculiar ecclesiastical court of the limits imposed by magistrates and more conservative bishops. Two more years later, Institutoris persuaded Sprenger, who was also a professor of theology in Cologne, to lend his name as co-author of a new treaty, Malleus Maleficarum (The Hammer of Warlocks), with which Institutoris hoped to recover part of the reputation lost because of its excesses.

Not content with getting Sprenger's collaboration, Institutoris also made it seem (apparently through forgery) that the prestigious theological faculty of Cologne endorsed the work, when in reality only four professors were willing to accept their extremism. It was not long before Institutoris and Sprenger quarreled, which was apparently something reasonable, and finally, after the Dominicans expelled him from Germany, the pope found a new mission for Institutoris in Eastern Europe. The tragic thing is that the Malleus, reprinted several times, and that it was a stylish book of medieval discussions, it became the classic reference for all who wanted to see sorcerers in his backyard. Skeptics found it more easy to ignore that refute ... and, after all, it had been printed including a papal and a letter of approval from the famous faculty of Cologne, capable documents of intimidating anyone.

The tastiest part of the book is the consideration of the belief that demons can function as sexual partners (the incubus and succubus) and of women, given the perversity of their nature and the insatiable nature of their lust, they were willing to accept the delights of those demonic loves. It's obvious that a woman who wants sexual contact with a fallen angel is capable of the most abominable crimes, but Institutoris specialized in painting his love of abortion and infant sacrifice, which was later used against many unfortunate midwives, when hysteria reaches its peak. In addition, sorcerers not only caused impotence (a recurring theme curiously in all the primitive literature about witchcraft), but they could even simulate castration in the unfortunate men who faced them. All that, added to the accustomed disasters of bad weather and the worst harvests. It should be noted that the term "synagogue" is not cited, probably because it is not yet gotten to penetrate in the German popular translation with which Institutoris was more familiar, but maybe also because it could have turned out counterproductive. The Inquisition, as conceived by that sexually obsessed Dominican, I was interested in discovering the women who had sexual relations with demons and that, in order to continue with their infernal loves, they agreed to act as instruments for the destruction of their Christians neighbors. Consequently, any personal setbacks, especially of sexual type, should be enough to encourage a "witness", whose anonymity was protected during the whole trial, to denounce a witch.

The witch hunts, as indicated by HR Trevor-Roper in his own analysis of the period, did nothing but inherit the logic of the pogroms that had devastated the same part of Germany at the beginning of the century in which the Malleus appeared. Particularly disturbing are the references to a "witch race", because of its suggestion that what could have been a voluntary transgression by the parents became a metaphysical stigma in the son which could be used calmly to justify the genocide. Brother Heinrich is a terrifying example of the kind of hysteria that we can wait whenever you start to rumble about a strange conspiracy. If there were a priest of our day, we would find him exciting the Knights of Colon locals against communist danger and writing profusely documented analysis about the subversive messages that can be found in rock music. The Inquisition, which was normally a research body, received a white letter from the pope, and with his deadly efficiency, Institutoris taught the West how to hunt the sorcerers. The French and German documents of the following two centuries bear witness to how the communities, again and again, decimate themselves and then reject with horror what they have done.

The Malleus presented the witches as sexually hungry, and, as HC Erick Midelfort points out in his own work on witch hunts, it was precisely in this period when he began to crumble the ancient concept of marriage and there were more single women who could provoke the suspicions of the officers in charge. When the hunt took off, single women were not the only victims or unfaithful as each victim had to confess who else had surrendered to the Devil. They formed lists that included men, women, children and the elderly. The innkeepers and the midwives were the ones most at risk of being named in a first round of accusations, but soon the owners and businessmen followed. Dissenting law enforcement officials, especially those who criticized those judicial proceedings, they were also easy targets for their colleagues, but often one of the pursuers fell into its own network. The confession of persecutor, named perhaps by suspects thirsty for revenge, used to be a precursor to a last burst of panic, before the community recognized the absurdity of his posture.

Even after this, it took years to disappear the factionalism caused by the judgments and among the reigning burn could still produce some new witch hunt. And all this in the name of religion and public order! It is important to note that despite the description we have of Heinrich Institutoris, most of the trials in Europe were not caused by the Inquisition and that this paid little attention to the extensive Malleus Maleficarum. Divisions that produced the Protestant Reformation in Christianity only served to strengthen the conviction of the French and German communities that the Devil was really intervening, in a new and scary way, in the human events. Protestants and Catholics, divided into doctrinal issues, agreed that those who had made a covenant with Satan had committed the worst human crime, something so horrible and so hidden that it justified the use of extraordinary procedures for its discovery.

No malicious action or physical assistance to a coven, it was as significant for the continental persecutors as the fact that someone, out of lust or greed, had given up his baptismal vows to become the prey of the devil. One of the most persistent ironies of the judgments is that confessions were accepted as safe indicators of the extent of diabolic activity within a community. Witches would repeatedly admit that they had been deceived by the Father of the Lies, because the gold that he had promised them became pieces of earthenware, or demonic loves were more painful than pleasers. Even the covens had to be considered possibly illusory. But when one-person, regardless of age or position, was named as a witch by several suspects had to face the torturers.

A suspect almost never stopped saying what was expected of him and the circumstances of their confession were used to reject any subsequent retraction. The only alternative - absolutely unacceptable to those pious men - would have been to admit the possibility that the judgments themselves were a lie. So far we have been talking about the development of the witchcraft legend in the regions of Europe where the persecutions of the Cathars and the Jews had already occurred. Among the various theories of how the madness of witchcraft began at the end of the fifteenth century, Trevor-Roper chose the idea that he represented the perennial conflict between the villagers of the plains and the population of the mountains, which was generally of different racial origin. Midelfort sees it as a consequence of the dislocations produced, in part, by the socioeconomic changes of the late Middle Ages and, in part, by the conflicts between Catholics and Protestants brought by the Reformation. And, of course, there are the old and now discarded theories that the judgments were result of clerical sexual frustrations or persecutor anxiety for confiscating the properties of the damned. What we should not forget is that the medieval idea of the witch had been evolving for centuries. At the beginning, it was the classic ugly old woman riding on a broom with a demon at her side in the form of a cat or toad. In the sixteenth century, this stereotype completely collapsed. In this new and dangerous era it was believed that the Devil could buy anyone's worship.

The great astronomer Kepler, for example, could not prevent his own mother's arrest for being a witch, who died in prison before the trial, perhaps fortunately for her. At the beginning of the century, a group of Ursuline nuns from a convent in Loudun showed some signs of demonic possession, and an unpopular priest, Urban Grandier, was executed like the sorcerer who had sold their souls to the devil. Yes, Satan was everywhere, even within the church itself. I agree with Midelfort's theory that witch hunts in general were the reflection of an insecurity, as the medieval era was giving way to the modern era, but a witch hunt could also occur simply because a community, knowing its existence everywhere, would have found evidence of having been attacked by the devil.

What happened in Salem, in the Massachusetts colony, is a good example. Less than fifty people died in America on charges of witchcraft, but twenty of them were from Salem in the horrendous panic of 1692. To understand Salem we must warn that, in the sixteenth and seventeenth centuries, England and its colonies seemed much less worried about witchcraft than continental Europe.

There was never, for example, concern for heresy that had become the substance of the continental judgments, and torture was not used to extract the kind of confessions that have perpetuated witch hunts in France and Germany.-The book of Chadwick Hansen, Witchcraft in Salem, is a late effort to rid the Massachusetts Puritan chiefs, especially Cotton Mather, of the charges formulated against them by non-sympathetic chroniclers. What happened, according to him, was that certain bungling in the field of divination caused hysterical reactions in a gang of teenagers. The initial accusation of witchcraft seemed justified when one of the women accused by the girls (Tituba, a Caribbean Indian slave) freely confessed his diabolism. The investigations that followed provided evidence that suggested that others who were later tried had practiced witchcraft, even reaching black magic, but this, in itself, would not have differentiated Salem - or its judgments - from any other American or English community.

What distinguished Salem was that the courts chose to accept the "spectral evidence" -the descriptions given by the girls of how they "saw" several community members trying malicious actions against them - against publicly expressed opinion by Cotton Mather, who had already successfully treated cases before of similar hysteria. Since hysteria mediates with attention, a certain number of men and women were charged, convicted and executed before the judges understood that those accusations that were multiplying, and that soon reached the most influential citizens of the community, they had to be false. This turn of opinion trampled the phenomena that had precipitated the trials, and the Salem's experience was a factor that influenced the renewal of English laws, that put an end to such persecutions. The sorcerers could still be arrested, but only as impostors.

Salem has now become a tourist attraction for those who wish to see the remains that remind us of that somewhat obscure chapter of American history. Some episodes of the Bewitched television series were filmed there to mix old and new legends, the medieval conception of the witch as a devotee of Satan and the Hollywood version, as a kind of funny superset. But the truth is that something ugly happened there, and not even with many laughs could the damage done in the name of God and the Crown be erased. All those comrades about the witches as consorts of the Devil went out of fashion with the emergence of a new scientific mentality. The judgments themselves had co-mentioned to fade even before that happened, as he became aware, as was the case in Salem, that the law was not the most appropriate vehicle to deal with what people called the supernatural.

In addition, as noted by Trevor-Roper, a general tendency towards less use of torture as a technique of interrogation meant that fewer confessions occurred and the less these abounded, the lower the likelihood of new ones occurring.

But in regions where ancient beliefs die slowly, as in the rural Devonshire area, which Tanya remembers so well, fear of witchcraft could still engender violence. Doreen Brave tells the story of a Devonshire farmer who attacked a woman he accused of having bewitched his pig. Your intentions had been drawing blood to break the spell and had threatened to kill her. That happened in 1924, but I have no doubt that today the same views hold true. Tanya was fortunate not to talk about her witchcraft when she was a child who attended the school in that region. She too could have been attacked. Even now we continually use pseudonyms, because we are not sure that someone, somewhere, won't blame her for any private setbacks she is experiencing. The American philosopher George Santayana once said that men who they ignore history, they are condemned to repeat their lessons. He suspects that the reverse is also true.

Often we need the experience of the present to understand the meaning of the past. The witch hunts of the late middle Ages can be considered a special version of the great spy hunts that occur whenever the towns begin to fear the subversion caused by a strong and cunning enemy. But psychology that caused them would not change, even if a new metaphysics replaced the old one. As Arthur Miller suggested in his work The Crucible, the fear of sabotage has not varied a lot, whether the scenario is the Salem of the seventeenth century or Washington. Only gods and devils vary. One of the least pleasant things about spy hunting is the way the behavior of the patriots mimic the supposed image of the enemy. We have, for example, the John Birch Society and the Minutemen, which are a copy of the most hateful characteristics of the Communist Party of the Soviet Union.

The same can be said of the dictatorships of Greece, Brazil or South Vietnam, when we read on tactics, which include indiscriminate arrests and often mortal torture, used to stop a real or imaginary communist threat. In England, in which in general the most macabre aspects of hunting for continental sorcerers, one of the most unpleasant characters that brought to the fore the general fear of witchcraft was a dark lawyer named

Mattew Hopkins, who, beginning in 1644, systematically terrorized Essex County with a pretend-issued by Parliament, where he was appointed General Discoverer of Warlocks. He offered his services by paying a fee and proved to be very skilled by obtaining confessions, without respecting the laws that prohibited the torture of suspects. Hopkins, who once claimed to be in possession of the Devil's payroll of althea witches of England (we can imagine standing before a people's court proclaiming "I have a list"), based his own image of the sorcerer on the volume written by King James I, shortly before his ascension to the throne of United England and Scotland.

Jacobo wanted his book Demonology to be a replica for skeptics like Reginald Scot, author of The Discovery of Witchcraft, and it brutalized the European witch image as Devil's lover. The Statutes of 1604, approved one year after Jacobo arrived in England, they broadened the definition of the actions that they constituted witchcraft and reinforced the penalties that should be applied. The king was gradually turning more and more skeptical, especially after witnessing a clear case of fraudulent spell, but his book and its laws were plagued by a later period. For Essex's lawyer they turned out to be a shortcut to fame and fortune. Following the descriptions given in Demonology, Hopkins spent two years hunting women whose pets could be taken by demons, sent to advise them on their hexes. In addition to employing the psychological torture of the continuous twenty-four hour interrogation revived the medieval ordeal to a suspicious witch, that is: throw the woman into a stream of water, to see if she floated or sank, assuming the Devil would prevent his servant from drowning. It was not long before their activities were interrupted by higher authorities, but, if we accept the old statistics, Hopkins became responsible for several hundred executions before he was called to answer for his illegal procedures and for the benefits he had obtained from his persecution of the witches.

One of the most curious aspects of the entire witch hunt period is that, from same way that fear of communist terror can be used to justify extraordinary political repression, the fear of magic was one of the things that induced citizens, who otherwise would have been fearful of God, to surrender to those practices prohibited in self-defense. Doreen Brave speaks, for example, of a glass-covered box, believed to be sold by Hopkins, as protection against witches and it contained some of the materials used in witchcraft. What people accepted normal, completely apart from the sermons on the intrinsic evil of the sorcery that they should hear in their parish church, was that the practice of witchcraft really existed ... and that seemed to work. Following the same mental process of the good Christians who borrowed money from Shylock, in The Merchant of Venice, of Shakespeare, it could be condemned to engage in a certain type of activity, but it was not taking advantage of that activity.

The pogroms, for example, ended when European Christians discovered that the Jews were "useful" and the only ones willing to deal with the prohibited but essential monetary loan practices in England, one of the factors that mitigated the witch hunt was that nobody apart of the most fanatical pursuers, he wanted to get rid of all the sorcerers, for fear of remaining defenseless before some new attack of the Spirit of Evil. Jeffrey Burton Russell, a historian who places the origins of witchcraft madness in the beliefs and practices of previous centuries, suggests that only 20 percent of the charges for witchcraft contained "theological refinements." The rest came from a popular tradition that theologians, including men like Institutoris, had rather learned than invented.

This is the tradition to which we must devote our attention to, if we want to penetrate the legends of the old and the new witchcraft, to find out what the truth of the witches in the past and how can this help us understand the possibilities that it has magic in the present.

The Truth About Sorcerers

We have examined two legends, one the reconstruction of the "Old Religion", by Margaret Murray and today's ritual groups; and the other, the medieval image of the devil, trampled by jealous persecutors who exceeded the limits of civil and ecclesiastical laws. Although Tanya does not accept the ritual group against as a vehicle suitable for its own magic, nor does it match the image of a consort of the devil, continues to describe herself as a witch. In this aspect, I have encouraged her and others, mainly because I lack another proper term as a substitute and because it implies a sense of tradition that I consider indispensable for effective magic.

What, then, is the true story of those we call sorcerers today? The legends we have already talked about always started from a European environment, and I will limit the following considerations to the West and especially to Celtic sources. Later we must discuss the meaning of magic in means other than Western, but, for now, it will suffice to indicate that there are few things in the tradition of Africa, Asia or the Americas that differ substantially from the traditions of Oldest Europe. Europe itself can be conceived as a beach to which they have gone to die successive tides, depositing each of them new materials. We don't know anything about the first, since the bulk of our archaeological evidence and all our written history is a product of the waves that came later. But towards the second millennium we can now locate these metaphorical tides with greater precision.

Some people, such as the Achaeans and the Etruscans, developed civilizations that they rivaled the oldest cultures of Egypt and Syria, with which they traded, but they melted in turn by pushing new villages north of the Black Sea. The Greeks and Romans invaded the peninsulas of the northern Mediterranean; Iranians and Aryans, the Middle East and the subcontinent of India, and the Celts, the intact territory of Western Europe. Once again, contact with the Egyptians and Phoenicians of Syria provided those new people of culture, which soon made them place themselves at the same level.

The Greeks used the Phoenician invention of the alphabet to preserve the memory of their cousins and Achaean predecessors in an incomparable literature, as well as to convert a decadent Egyptian theology in the remarkable new vision of man we find in the philosophies of Pythagoras and Plato. The Romans, who were great organizers, more than writers, like the Greeks, they crushed their Etruscan rivals, they destroyed the power of Phenicia (the former ally of the Etruscans) in its colony of Carthage, north of Africa, and then they moved forward, first to annex Greece and then to the rest from the Mediterranean. But the organization has its drawbacks. The Romans, who were forced to deal with the threat of a Celtic invasion, according to the people of the region known as Gaul was being pushed south by its Teutonic relatives. They began to admire the value of their enemies. In sharp contrast to the indulgence that seemed a natural consequence of their successes, they saw the Celts, living in intimate contact with nature and with much more honesty in your personal relationships.

Julius Caesar, for example, he wrote about the Druids, the Celtic priests, calling them philosophers that encouraged the Gallic warriors to reach new tops of bravery, with a vision of reincarnation; and Tacitus, a century later, spoke of the Celtic exploits in what would convert the primitive version of the myth of the Noble

Wild. The writers of the eighteenth and nineteenth centuries would accept these two versions of the Celts, by seeming incompatible: that of authentic primitive beings, and that of their mystical character. The result was a lot of meaningless works, which anticipated the romanticism of Margaret Murray and Gerald Gardner and led to the appearance of reconstructed druidic orders, even before there were ritual groups rebuilt. The truth about the Celtic religion, which I accept at the same time as the truth about the first European sorcerers, is that it reflected a much less barbaric culture than Tacitus tells us, but also much less sophisticated than Caesar intends. The Celts had already established contact with other cultures, through their trade with the Etruscans, and shortly before the beginning of the Christian era they were in a position analog us to that of the Indian tribes challenged by the English settlers on the Atlantic shore.

There were enough villages and communications to allow the possibility of a new national unity, but the process was still incomplete. In the same way as the European intrusion prevented the Iroquois from becoming North America in a unique power, Roman intrusion destroyed the nascent nationalism of the various Celtic people. One of the main combats of this conflict took place in the Anno Domini 61, in Anglesey, when Roman Paulino underwent a British Druid center, despite the efforts of women dressed in black screaming trying to get their troops to withdraw. It is not known for sure how powerful the Druids were in England. There is absolutely no proof, for example, to relate the Druids to the ruins of Stonehenge, and, despite the assumption of Caesar that his center was in England, it was possible that he did little for them to arrive from the continent. What we know is that they formed a priestly house in Gaul, which shared the privileges of a heroic aristocracy with warriors. It is very possible that the uniformity of a ritual education, through a period that could include up to two decades, I would have already developed in the Druids a sensitivity towards interests that they transcended the limited concerns of any of the tribes.

One of the factors that could have helped the Druids to get a certain Celtic unity was the cult of the god Cernunos ("The Cuckold"), which had an acceptance that was going beyond the regional. This pastoral divinity was conventionally represented with antennas or horns and accompanied by a deer and a ram-headed snake. Legends about Cernunos describe him as the lord of animals. In Celtic art this god appears sitting squatting among several animals. Also appears as lord of the underworld and, consequently, as a source of wealth for his worshipers. For the Romans, the suppression of the Druidic cult of Cernunos was important, for purely political reasons. With the advent of Christianity, the Horned God will encounter new and stubborn enemies. Squatting images were adopted of Cernunos to represent the Devil, and the stories in which Cernunos appeared as the huge black lord of beasts became part of folklore concerning the way the Devil was seen by his followers.

It should be noted that the black color was the way of representing the supernatural; for the Celts, the death color was red. Other gods and goddesses ran better luck among Christians than Cernunos. The best example is the triple Brigantia (the High), or Brígida, a Celtic mother goddess, associated with frequency by the Romans to Minerva, which became in Santa Brígida de Kildare. Attributes of other deities were endorsed to prestigious saints, like the monk Columba, who was said to know the language of the birds and that he had a white horse that predicted the death of his owner. Minor local divinities, such as figures originally revered as Protectors of wells and rivers, became the fairies, of which theologians would say that they were minor demons or souls of the unbaptized. Even a great Pastoral festival, like Samuin (November 1), was Christianized and become the All Saints Day.

According to Roman accounts, the Druids practiced animal and human sacrifices and we know that the cult of the severed head was the most common expression of the Celtic religion. But there is nothing that supports Margaret Murray's claim that the Celtic priests practiced the cult of Cernunos by dressing so that they will resemble him, nor is there anything that suggests the existence of ritual groups of sorcerers as a kind of religious bureaucracy. Cernunos is also represented occasionally naked, as the god of war (the Celts fought naked in a demonstration of courage against their enemy battleships), but there is also no reason to believe that the Celtic festivals required that their participants not carry more than "the layer of heaven." The bloody festivals of wandering bands of warriors do not fit well with the image of the coven that finally developed in medieval tradition, and it seems that it can be safely stated that the image of the "synagogue" or "coven" is part of 20 percent of the tradition of witchcraft that is strictly clerical invention.

Even the number thirteen, associated with that word "coven", is a ritual group consisting of thirteen sorcerers. We should not forget that the term is just a variant of the word "convent". How I had to know the Scottish witch who introduced the term in his confession, religious groups, like the Franciscans, preferred to keep their communities or convents with a number as close as possible to the one they formed Jesus and his twelve apostles. In medieval trials, no one was ever set a specific composition for "synagogues". Although the change from human to animal form by some kind of enchantment is an occasional motive in Greco-Roman mythology. Among the Celts is the fundamental characteristic of a doctrine in which the world of birds and animals and that of men intersect continuously.

It is also the origin of the belief in vampirism, which the Celts shared with the Greeks and the Romans. The warrior goddesses, particularly those who adopted the shape of crows, they could attack their enemies and tear them apart literally. In Greece they were monsters, which were called lamiai; in Rome, lamiae or strigae (derived from the word that was used to designate an owl). Later tradition would vulgarize these supernatural beings somewhat by pretending them as ghost blood suckers, trying to regain their lost vitality. In the Christian era, what had been a fearsome feature of the pagan goddesses finally became one of the accusations thrown against the old helpless that fit the witch's first stereotype. The witch's cauldron, which will be familiar to any Macbeth reader, is another example of Celtic folklore reduced to a convenient scale.

In the myths are found references to a cauldron of immortality. Also, and since the Celts revered water more than any other element, It was natural that the cubes and Cauldrons also had their role in their conception of a good spell. "Bulle and bubble, work and confuse." Although the worldly power of the Druids succumbed in their struggles with the Romans, they survived for several centuries of the Christian era by transmitting knowledge lies, that even in purely secular terms, the local lords found superior to the instruction of the first Christian priests they had known.

The development in Scotland of an order of highly intellectualized monks, with the Columba of the sixth century, meant that the Druids, who were already very close to the extinction, they would no longer enjoy the advantage that their poetry gave them, against Christian priests who knew Latin and Greek literature. The myth became a folklore that Christians themselves incorporated, for their own purposes, and the magic of the gods and goddesses went through a process of infantilization, to sprout again as a set of rural superstitions about healings and divination. Witchcraft itself was not yet a source of terror for Christians. Quite the opposite. Charlemagne, who was crowned ruler of the new Holy Roman Empire on Christmas Day of the year 800, reinforced in its capitulates the prohibitions against the belief in ancient magic, like the Canon Episcopi of which we have already spoken.

True sorcerers - beings capable of performing marvelous actions with the only help from their own powers - they could not exist nor did they exist. Despite these official denials, there was a Germanic folklore in which echoes of the walking troops of warriors of a less settled era. According to these stories, a spirit, usually a goddess named Perchta or Holda, identified with the Roman Diana, it led to a horde of spirits in a wild hunting, which caused the destruction of everyone who crossed their path. With time, those supernatural hunters were considered real people, to whom the goddess had conferred the power to fly - the belief that the Canon was trying to suppress Episcopi. But in a short period of time, belief in Diana gave way to belief in the Devil, and one of the components of the myth of the coven was established when the medieval clergy decided that Satan had the power to instantly transport his followers to any place. After all, Diana doesn't know it existed, and the heresy that rejected the Canon Episcopi was to attribute to a deity Pagans wonderful powers.

The Devil was something completely different, and now the heresy consisted rather in denying its ability than in affirming it. It was always taken for granted that the Devil was not an independent entity of God. According to the Christians, Satan's attacks were to be considered evidence for the righteous, spoiled by the Lord. The basic text here was the Book of Jacob. The Wizards - people who accepted Satan's mandates, for whatever reason - were guilty of treason crime against the true lord of the world, that although the orgies to which wizards attended were pure hallucinations, a hoax devised by the Devil to catch the wicked. At this point the legend and history intersect in a very curious way. In the Judgment literature, you can read stories of voluntary confessions over and over again where suspects claimed to have assisted the covens, even when there existed evidence that they had been sleeping.

For those who believed in malevolent witches, this introduced the idea of "spectral evidence", as in the Salem trials, in that those who had engaged in evil practices had been the astral bodies of the accused. But for the skeptics it represented the opportunity to comment about the unusual properties of ointments used by sorcerers. Since the Aconite, belladonna and hemlock are among the drugs mentioned in the traditional recipes to fly and change shape, skeptics seemed right to affirm that the only "trips" made by the witches were those caused by the ointments.

In my opinion, the question lies in knowing to what extent they were used. Except for Margaret Murray and her followers, almost all the students of the history of witchcraft have agreed to attribute the non-forced confessions that appear in the literature of the subject to mental disorders. The fantastic descriptions of the covens, for example, have been considered hysterical responses to coldness and repression that characterized medieval life. But it could also be that it was expressions of a subculture of drugs, rooted either in ancient times or in the most recent experiments of people considered rural pharmacologists. I venture this hypothesis with great reservations.

John M. Allegro, in The Sacred Mushroom and the Cross, had already expressed his bold opinion that much of the mythology of the ancient world, including the stories of the Old and New Testaments, reflects a cult of drugs and fertility, in which the hallucinogenic mushroom Amanita was used (called in agaric Europe). According to Allegro, this cult was still valid in the 1st century of the Christian era. The authorities of the nation; Christian community, ignorant of the true origins of the sect to which they had converted, they accepted documents like the gospels and epistles for their face value, rather than as initiation in code of the secrets of the cult.

Heretics as the Gnostics followed wrapping up that truth, but they were cruelly suppressed over time. I differ from Allegro's basic thesis, but I must admit at the same time that I could. There is an undercover cult of drugs in the ancient world. It is possible that the foundation of poisons, which was related to witchcraft in the old imperial order, will include the science of how to use those substances in limited doses, or by external applications, to create hallucinogenic effects. This science could be transmitted within a very limited and formal organization and arrive more or less intact until the Middle Ages. Apart from whether the skill in hallucinogen composition was somewhat ancient, or relatively recent, apparently it is a fact that existed in the Middle Ages.

Memories of the ancient practices of Celtic worship, many of which had endured in various popular practices, as well as a distorted understanding of Cathars, they were able to provide the basis for private reveries that, in a state of abnormal consciousness, they could assume the form of a "separate reality", totally satisfactory. This could be a much less spiritual experience than the ecstasy approved by the medieval church, but highly functional for the men and women who lived in the Margins of the society of the Middle Ages. And what about the most disgusting ingredients in recipes, such as the Babies body fat, or children's bone marrow? Most likely is that they are fantasies of demonologists, but it is possible that they are individuals who accepted the need for useful substances and cases could cause infanticide or tomb rape to get them.

I repeat that all this is nothing more than pure conjecture. The only reason that interest in this aspect of medieval sorcerers, as adherents to a cult of drugs, is because I am aware of the role that these substances have played in the occult from more recent times.

Aleister Crowley shocked his former colleagues in the Golden Dawn for its own acceptance of opium and cocaine as legitimate adjuvants in the practice of magic, and the resuscitation of more autonomous witchcraft towards the end of the 1960s it is closely related to the use of drugs for the young. The same could happen in the middle Ages.

The Celtic religion flourished in an environment in which he drank incredibly, and the Greek Dionysian cult - which was itself same a hidden religion, which coexisted with the most respectable temple cults-demanded alcohol as a vehicle for ecstasy. Couldn't have worked the same mode a systematic use of hallucinogens for even less orthodox groups in worlds of Greek and Celtic magic? Even if there is what to support this hypothesis, it should be remembered that beliefs and Greek practices were so desperate that there was nothing that seemed a long way from a universal worship. The poet Robert Graves, for example, has expressed the opposite idea that there was a cult of the "White Goddess" throughout ancient Europe, and, following Margaret Murray, that the medieval witch ritual groups kept this alive until a later time.

Of course, it is true that there is a lunar motif in Greek folklore, in triplicity of Artemis-Selene-Hecate (the crescent moon, the full moon and the waning moon) and that Celtic representations of a mother goddess (the Magna Mater) resembled this Greek image. But the Celts used to be supporters of triads. Also, unlike their Greek opponents, Celtic mother goddesses are sometimes represented with the attributes that accredit them as goddesses of the hunt – a vital characteristic of the cult of Diana, as interpreted by the members of Modern ritual groups. If not even the Druids, Cernunos' servers, made an appearance in the whole Celtic world, the existence of an extended matriarchal cult, that was dedicated to Diana's Celtic equivalent, it seems very unlikely.

I tend to share Jeffrey Burton Russell's idea about the medieval image of the witch as a gradual humanization of the characteristics of the ancient Celtic deities. There is no doubt that there was a lot of sorcery in the Celtic world. Regardless of the arts practiced by the tribal shamans we know with the name of druids. I think this witchcraft survived the fall of the Druids already preaching of the Christian priests. Most likely, its practitioners were mostly women, who were excluded from the Druidic and Christian ministries. During the Middle Ages, those witches, who had to keep their secret practices because of prohibitions, they would be Christian, but with a Christianity full of strong Celtic reminiscences.

As with the voodoo of Haiti, even the language of the sorcery had to change to reflect the official beliefs that replaced the more primitive religion of a subjugated people, but witchcraft itself meant a mythical structure extracted from an almost forgotten era. Ironically, and again as in Haiti, the customs of a missing priesthood would be preserved by individuals that at an earlier time would have been excluded from such ministry. So then it is correct to speak of the "Old Religion", but not precisely in the sense that it gives Margaret Murray. It is obvious that there were many other influences in the conformation of the witchcraft of the Middle Ages. The legend developed by the persecutors, introducing a vision of the world in Cathar terms, he was able to push the sorcerers themselves to replace Cernunos by the Devil, in his memory of a Celtic past. Although in these circumstances he saw the Devil as a friend of humanity and not as his implacable adversary.

Another influence was the tradition of ceremonial magic, reintroduced in the West by those who were familiar with their continuity in the hybrid culture of the world Islamic. The magical texts, for example, were a clear cup of Celtic witchcraft, although the magicians, who were generally men from an urban environment and intellectual, they interpreted their sorcery as a manipulation of hidden powers of nature and not as the erotic cult of the devil attributed to ignorant peasants. But, over time, bits of science from those treaties may have mixed with Celtic practices, in a way that reinforced the image of the sorcerer as the demonic powers. Meanwhile, a potentially condemnatory element had been introduced into the tradition of what witches could and could not do. It was the idea that the soul of a sorcerer could separate, in a way, from his body to assist the covens.

The concept of the Lamia or Striga of Greco-Roman folklore was applied to the sorcerers in general. It was no longer about changing shape, as in lycanthropy, but in the insidious action of the astral or spectral body of the sorcerer. Even with this idea, there was the conviction that the demoniacs were people infested by strange powers worshiped by sorcerers. Through the ceremonies related to exorcism, the haunted could be forced to reveal the provenance of the evil that afflicted him. He might even be able to witness what happened to the Spectral body of the sorcerer, regardless of what was known about the location or activities of your physical body.

In Loudun, in the 1630s, a hysterical French prioress, Soeur Jeanne des Anges, convinced enough people responsible that she was possessed to provoke the arrest of a priest, Urban Grandier, who had won enmity of the main citizens of Loudun. During the trial, the judges heard testimonies that assured that the priest, despite being imprisoned, had been able to still attack the nuns in their convent. Condemned by sorcier (sorcerer), Grandier was tortured and then burned alive. Soeur Jeanne, whose frantic retraction had been considered by the judges as one more proof of the intensity of his possession, he was finally released from his demons and became a kind of celebrity in the court of Louis XIII. The son of the king, the future Louis XIV, was born with the nun's shirt, which was said to be miraculous.

Before we examine further the complex tradition that was developing in the Mediterranean world even while the Druids were in full decline. In the following chapters we will penetrate deeper into the world of Hellenistic magic, the source of the greatest part of the knowledge that sorcerers accept as inheritance, without knowing its true origin. It is the world of astrology and alchemy, and also the world of ceremonial magic. It is even more than Tanya's world or that of the "elf arts" of the Celts. And with his I think that we can also begin to understand something else about the true meaning of occultism, in the development of Western thought, including even the scientific point of view that, by definition, might seem completely opposite to everything that it is understood by magic.

The Creation Of The Myths In Wicca

Nobody knows where the myths in Wicca come from, the only certainty is that they come from the ancient Celts, who invented stories about events, or fanciful stories, so as to pass the beliefs from generation to generation. Most of the Myths are mostly descriptions of the performance of the various aspects of the gods, and other important characters in religion. You cannot find a book of myths that is unique and true, since mythology itself is a personal experience of wiccans, either alone or in a circle, with the gods.

Among the mythologies, the best known is that of Merlin, which is known even by those who are not practitioners of the ancient religion. From these myths come most of the symbols of our rituals, since these are a representation of all the myths and beliefs of Wicca. We will see this more carefully when we study the Sabbats. What we should keep in mind, in relation to Wicca, is that we can ALL write our myths and our beliefs about the gods. There is no conception since wicca is not a religion of the book, but rather a religion of personal EXPERIENCE with the gods.

The Gods

In the same way, we know that there are stereotypes about deities, but these are not because they are the only accepted conception of them, which differentiates us from other religions of the world. The wicca has its personal conception of the gods and above all it has the freedom to be able to worship any of the gods, be their character with which you feel more at ease. About what we call the gods, well, there are common names known by the most pagans, appointed according to the character and personality of God which is evoked. But that doesn't deprive us of being able to change their name and use the name.

For example, I know people who, to avoid persecution in extremely Catholic families, they saw the need to change the names of the gods for Jesus and Mary; with which prevented their relatives from persecuting them. And they could even pray together, just they were actually praying to different gods. In addition to common names, there are the "secret" names of the gods that are with which the coven called within the circle, and is only revealed to the initiated. When we study the Sabbats we will see how the facets of these gods govern over every part of the year and why.

THE EXISTENCE PLANS

The existence of other worlds or dimensions is part of many hidden traditions. Wicca has been influenced by many Eastern philosophies about this, but it has retained the pre-Christian concepts of the Old Religion. The three planes of where all things emanate, seen in the ancient Greek texts and then in the Celtic tradition. They are still part of many Wicca traditions. Other Wiccan groups have fully embraced the Seven Plans of Existence common to Oriental concepts, which do not go according to the Three Planes principle. There are also groups that have incorporated Western Occultism into Wicca. We will focus on the concept of these plans according to Modern Wicca.

THE ASTRAL PLANE

An integral aspect of the Wicca Mysteries is that of the Astral Plane. This is one dimension that is not easily defined since it is compressed into various realities and comparisons .It can be said that it is a continuous parallel between space and time. It is also a state of consciousness, related to the imagination, but more within the kingdom controlled by mental images, which the controlled by simple thoughts or sounding awake. Where the Physical Plane is the Plane of Form, the Astral Plane is the Plane of the Force.

The world of dreams is one of the doors to the Astral World. In the teachings of mysteries, the initiate is instructed in the control of his dreams. Once programmed and prepared, the Dream can be conducted and directed, then the portal to the astral world is opened by which the initiate can enter and leave at ease and will. Some initiates prefer to establish a temple in the world of dreams, from which they can transfer the influences to the Astral world, without having to really enter the same.

The matter of the Astral world is known as Astral Light. It can be modeled and molded like clay, through the energy of our emotions and feelings. It is in this etheric substance that we create beings known as "Way of Thought" (thought-forms) that serve as channels to greater forces. This matter is not only influenced by the emanations of the physical dimension, but also for those from Higher Dimensions, including the Divine and Spiritual kingdoms. In this way the events and situations generated by superior plans, take shape in the astral plane, and manifest in the physical plane (unless that other energy alters them in some way). It is here where the Art of Divination comes in. It is based on metaphysical science. If a person can catch images that they are forming on the astral plane, then they can discern what is being manifest on the physical plane.

We must understand however that divination is the art of anticipating the events that are about to manifest. The Astral images that are encouraging or giving life to that event can be altered by the constant flow of emotions that pass through the astral dimension. Therefore, what we see in Divination is what will happen if the patterns remain unchanged. In the Hidden

Teachings, nothing is fixed in time, nothing will happen in our lives even if we don't want to (except the death of the physical body). However, the biggest events in our lives are part of the patterns printed on our spirits when our souls are born in a physical body.

This is the metaphysical basis of Astrology, also called Astral or Stellar Impression. Our natal (or astral) chart shows the major patterns drawn for us in every physical life, as well as the strength and weakness of our spiritual state. We can work and change them because we have free will.

THE ELEMENTARY PLANE

The Teachings of the Mysteries, or Occult Teachings, also include the Elemental Plane or Plane of the Forces. This plane represents the actions of the four creative forces or elements, which comprise everything that manifests and is shaped in the physical dimension. Examining these elements and the process by which the manifestation takes place, there is the fifth element known as Spirit. This Etheric element is superior to the four elements. If we say that the four Elements mark the points of the circle, the fifth is the circle itself!

Earth is the solid element and represents the metaphysical concept of the Law. Air is the element of the Intellect and represents the Metaphysical concept of Life. Fire is the element of action and represents the metaphysical concept of Light. Water is the element of fertility and represents the metaphysical concept of love. The various aspects of the Elemental Plane are intertwined with everything Wiccan does or Experiments in your life. In magic, they are wrapped in spells, invocations, consecration of amulets, tools, and the circle itself. In a metaphysical sense, they reflect the psyche and emotions of Wiccan.

The personality of the individual and any emotional instability is directly proportional to the balance of the nature of the elements that reside in that person. The awareness of these elements is known as manna, numen or more commonly as elementals. The elementals of the earth are spirits whose vibration is so close to that of the Earth itself, which alter its mineral composition, also have power over rocks, flora and fauna. The elementals of the air are the spirits whose vibration is intimately related to the energy emanated by electro impulses of all living beings. They also have power over the mind and nervous system.

The elementals of fire are the spirits whose ranges of vibration are very similar to emotional energies, such as being joy, love, hate, fear and other powerful emotions. They also have power over emotions and the general state of the body's metabolism. The elementals of water are the spirits whose vibrations are similar to fluids. They have power over the balance between the moisture and fluids, and the rest of nature.

All creation is animated and influenced by the presence of these elements (or the lack thereof). Every object that suffers a manifestation shares a material and a spiritual nature. Material nature shapes it, and spiritual nature gives it life. However, everything physical has its spiritual counterpart. The metaphysical correspondences of the elements are contained in the Zodiac and they help to prepare the astral chart. Empedocles, a student of Pythagoras, was the first to introduce the doctrine of the Four Elements and insert it into Astrology. He taught in his homeland of Sicily around 475 BC, presenting the four elements like the quadruple root to all things. This is the traditional picture in the European occultism derived from his teachings:

Earth: Taurus, Virgo, Capricorn
Cold + Dry Air: Gemini, Libra, Aquarius
Hot + Wet Fire: Aries, Leo, Sagittarius
Hot + dry Water: Cancer, Scorpio, Pisces
Cold + Wet SUMMERLAND (Summer Country) Summerland is a term generally used by Wiccans to describe the other World or Beyond, to which the souls of the dead go to the end of their physical life. It could

be considered as a kind of paradise, not unlike the Land of Happy Hunting belonging to some indigenous traditions.

Summerland exists in the astral plane and is experienced in different ways by each individual, according to the spiritual vibrations that he carries to that plane of existence. How long one stays there? It depends on each one's ability to release and resolve the burden that each one carries from life to life, causing to be the object of a reincarnation in the physical plane. The existence in the Summerland allows each individual the opportunity to learn and understand the lessons of previous life and how they relate to previously experienced lives by that soul.

In Wiccan theology it is called "time of rest and recovery." Once that period has passed, the Elemental Plane begins to stretch the individual towards a reincarnation, whatever the dimension in harmony with the spiritual condition of the individual. The reincarnation of the soul is subject to the plane of forces, and can be poured into the vortex of a sexual union that takes place in the Physical Plane. In the hidden teachings it is said that the soul is poured into the physical plane that will best prepare you for the lessons you need to learn in the path of evolution for the final liberation of the reincarnation cycle. In the Hidden Teachings, a loss of pregnancy indicates that the soul of that creature is no longer needed to return to the physical world, but he only needed a small appearance in physics matter in order to balance the etheric elementary properties required for its spiritual body.

The other reason for that to happen is that parents needed that lesson in order to evolve spiritually, in that case a soul that did not need to reincarnate or have physical existence. That soul is known not only in this area, but in others as being the teachings of the incarnation of higher spirits like that of Buddha or Jesus.

THE HIDDEN DIMENSIONS

Hidden philosophies hold that there are four kingdoms that encompass creation: Spiritual, Mental, Astral and Physical. For the purposes of this book we will only analyze the interior dimensions, since these functions as part of the internal mechanism of the Mysteries. Just as there are physical planes of existence, there is also the spiritual plane. It is believed that each plane is a reflection of the upper plane. The occult saying, "How is it top down" originates from this concept.

Essentially every immediate inferior plane manifests the "Thought Form" created in the immediate superior plane. In magic, one establishes his desire on the higher plane so that it manifests in the bottom plane. The seven planes are as follows.

1- Last Dimension
2- Divine Dimension
3- Spiritual Dimension
4- Mental Dimension
5- Astral Dimension
6- Elemental Dimension (Plan of the Forces)
7- Physical Dimension (Plane of Forms)

Directly on the plane of forms is the elementary plane. Everything that happens in the physical plane is closely related to this plane. Dimensions react like a row of domino pieces; one pushes the other and the chain starts. This is a law of physics, and also Metaphysics (as above is below) and it is how magic spells work. This law is the internal mechanism that works within the planes. Each plane vibrating as a consequence of the vibrations received from another plane.

Above the plane of the forces is the Astral plane, which is an ethereal realm that contains the "forms of thought" of collective consciousness. It is here where the heavens and hells of Religious beliefs exist, fueled by the thoughts and Religious emotions of the physical plane. In this plane we can create images of what we want what we fear. From the moment we all have a bit of the creative spark that created us. We can use that same force.

Our creative minds operate the someway. The consciousness that gave us life works, the only difference being is that we are a spark and not the source. The creative process of all ways is practically the same that we use to create magic. For example, if I decide to create a pulpit that will hold papers during a speech. First of all I need to create it in my mind. That thought will go through the different states represented by the seven planes. The divine plane will receive the spark of the Latest plane. The spiritual plane will conceive the plane, the mental will visualize it, the astral will create it in etheric matter, the elementary will bring the way of thinking and the physical plane will provide the substance ... and abracadabra ... we have the pulpit!!!

In simple terms, the need above and I begin to think that I need to satisfy that need and I eventually form an idea and then I refine the idea so that I can see it in my mind. Once I can see it clearly with the mind's eye, I draw it on a paper. Then gather the necessary materials for construction and I begin to assemble it. Once finished assembling I have the required object and my work is finished.

Magic is an art of creation. The material we use is the Astral substance. The power to create with our thoughts resides in us because of the creative Spark. We create according to the divine formula of the planes. Major is the emotion, more exact being to the thought, and thus also its corresponding response of the Astral Plane. In order to create changes in the physical world (magically) first we must cause them in the astral plane. The purpose of the magic ritual is to raise and direct the energy (which contains the form of thought) to the Astral Plane. The symbols, gestures, colors and elements of the ritual are all methods of astral communication. They also create the necessary images so that all participants come together and form a collective conscience.

Each releases a load of vibrations to the magic ritual. The ways of thinking begin to manifest in the astral plane and become channels for superior forces. The ritual energizes those forms; the channels then open in response to that and the forces become more powerful. Then, according to the work and its nature, the raised energy will rise to the Astral Plane, or descend from the divine plane (in the case of invocation rituals of the gods)

THE WICCA CODE

The name of WICCA is given, to the contraction of the English term WITCHCRAFT and whose root is WICCA celtic. It means women priestesses who then will be called witches. The name of Wicca religion is given to the mother of all magic that bases her beliefs in the powers of nature: the wiccan motto or Wicca religion, the governing principle simply state: "feel free to share the arts of magic, develop and use your being to be psychic and do what you want, provided that the result does not cause harm to nobody".

WHAT IS FORBIDDEN?

Initiates consider it imperative to keep the Wiccan motto in mind before performing any ritual, especially those that may be considered lacking in ethics or manipulative in nature. They ensure that if you violate it even unintentionally, an instant is generated bad for karma, so you have to be very careful and think twice before using magic or psychic powers to take revenge on an enemy.

WHAT IS ALLOWED?

If you think it is necessary, feel free to make changes or minor additions in any spell (herbs, oils, incense, etc.) can be substituted for others materials as long as the magical properties remain the same, however not change the moon phase in which the spell is to be performed or the results thereof are affected. Finally, after making a spell, you should thank the Goddess for its presence and protection; followed by a ritual of de-meditation to relax.

WHAT IS RECOMMENDED TO DO?

It is recommended to always take care of problems using positive magic energy and without concentrating on the negative. The old sorceresses also say that if you deliberately harm or manipulate another person with magic or another form of evil, you will pay for it by receiving triple the desired evil. Reason - whenever a help spell is done to others, a result will be obtained good karma.

THE WICCAN LAWS

1. If you don't harm anyone, do what you want
2. If you know that the Rede is being broken, you must work hard against it.
3. Look, listen and keep your judgment, in the debates, let your silence be long, your thoughts clear and your words well-chosen
4. Never run over, threaten or speak ill of anyone
5. Be True Always, so in speaking you will avoid great evils
6. Never haggle over the price of your Tools
7. Keep your body, your clothes and your house clean
8. Do not take a task that you will not be able to complete, and if you take any, hard work to fulfill it correctly in the established time.
9. Reverence, honor, care and heal the Earth

10. Of what you grow, use what you need and leave as much as possible to return to Earth as an offering, as a way of nourishing the cycle of life

11. Do not judge those of other paths, but offer them love and help

12. Do not steal from humans, animals or spirits; if you have needs you can't supply, return to your community.

13. Offer friendship and hospitality to strangers who come to visit

14. Never join or marry someone you don't love

15. Honor the unions and commitments of others, and do not have relationships with someone if that will cause harm to another person

16. Raise your children with kindness, feed them, dress them, and take them home as much as you can. Show them your love and affection. Teach them strength and wisdom.

17. You will not have slaves, nor will you participate in any organization, state or community that allows these practices

18. Be fair and honest in all your transactions with others, fulfilling the letter and the spirit of each contract you make.

19. The High Priests will rule the Coven as representatives of the gods.

20. The High Regent Priests will choose who they will have per second, once proven that these have sufficient rank.

21. Within the Circle, the commands and wishes of the High Priests are Law

22. The High Priests command their role as Magicians, Counselors and Fathers

23. If there is a dispute between you, let the High Priests summon the elders, who after hearing both sides together and separately, will issue a judgment

24. If the High Priests find it necessary to punish, suspend or expel any member, this must be done in private and accepted gracefully by the member

25. He who does not like to work under the High Priests, will look for another Coven, or will find another if it has the necessary range. He and every member who wants to go with him, they should avoid any contact with the old Coven for a period of time, until the Covens form a harmonious relationship bond again.

26. If one of the High Priests leaves Coven and returns within the period of his regency, he must be accepted again as if nothing had happened. If you do not return,

you must name Sumo again to the one who was supplying the one who retired; unless there are reasons valid to prevent that.

27. High Priests must withdraw from office with grace to make way for new High Priests, after the period established by the Council

28. Any High Priest who consents to the breaking of the Rede must be expelled

29. Before Coven performs the magic, a consensus must be made so that everyone agrees that no one will be damaged.

30. The circle must be duly conjured and purified. The Wiccan must be prepared and purified to enter the circle

31. No one can tell outsiders when or where Coven will meet, without the consent of the Coven Council

32. Don't gossip or talk badly about anyone in Wicca

33. Never lie to the Elders or anyone from Wicca

34. No one but those of Wicca will see the hidden mysteries; but with the consent of the council, family or friends can witness the ceremony

35. No one should reveal to outsiders who Wiccan is, or give names or any other data that could endanger the Arts, or lead it to face the laws of the country, or with those who persecute them.

36. Keep in your book of shadows the teachings of your Coven, as well as your rituals and the things you learned

37. No one can enter the circle with those in enmity. In a dispute No one can evoke any other law than that of Wicca, or any other authority other than High Priests and the Elders.

38. It's okay to receive money for what you do with your hands but not for what you do perform within a circle Never accept money for the use of magic, or for the teachings of the arts within the circle.

39. Never use magic to show yourself, for pride.

40. Contribute with your talents, your work and your earnings with Coven, and with causes Nobles who honor the Gods. Honor those who work voluntarily at arts service without receiving anything in return.

41. Never do anything to dishonor the Gods or the Wicca

Statement Of Purpose

Our purposes are those of

:1. Live in a way that honors the Gods, following the Wiccan Network

2. Explore and practice Wiccan beliefs and traditions, with the main focus towards the traditions of the British Isles

3. Support each other within Coven in terms of health, growth and aspirations

4. Fulfill the Wiccan Rituals corresponding to the Sabbats, Esbats and special events, to celebrate the seasons, perform magic, recognize the rites of passage, and honor the Gods

5. Honor the Earth and all its creatures as sacred; and work to heal and protect the environment in our community.

6. Teach Wiccan beliefs and traditions to members and students, siblings and sisters of the arts, or anyone who is open to various spiritual paths

7. Commitment

8. All members of this Coven must be deeply committed to living their beliefs, and devote themselves fully to fulfilling these purposes in their activities and in their lives.

Membership Qualification

Membership will be offered to individuals on the recommendation of the High Priest or High Priestess, the approval of the Council and the consensus of the Initiates (members assets) of Coven. No one can be denied membership based on their gender, race, ethnic background, sexual preference, physical disability or age (proving that they are adults).

Degrees Of Participation And Membership

Participants in the activities carried out by this Coven include the following:

1. Guests: interested persons who can participate in the open activities, or closed from Coven in the company of an initiate, with the consent of the rest of the Initiates

2. Congregants: people who consider themselves Wiccan and participate and support the Coven open activities.

3. Dedicators: people who have been dedicated to the study of the Wicca path, with the approval of all active Initiates who are being instructed in the arts. Then once the time is established for the initiation, the person can request it or withdraw from the Coven without obligations. Membership in Coven is reserved for:

I - Initiates: People who, having been active in Coven, or on the Wicca way, after trying it and having spent a year and a day, they have fulfilled all the requirements of the Coven Council for initiation and were initiated Priests of the gods.

II - Second Degree Initiates: People who have been active in Coven, or in the walk (having tried it) for two years and two days, and have fulfilled the requirements for the Second Degree Initiation, having been recommended byte High Priests, and approved by the consensus of the Initiates.

III - Third Degree Initiates: People who, having acquired the Second Degree, have demonstrated skill in creating rituals, leadership, teaching, counseling group processes and administration; and have been recommended by the High Priests and approved by the consensus of the Initiates. Additional recognition titles: The Titles of Teacher in the Arts will be granted to those who acquire specific achievements. First Grade Initiates who have achieved efficiency in certain disciplines, having been approved and tested by the consensus of the Initiates of Second Degree and those of Third Degree, will receive the Title of Teacher in the Arts, these may be:

1. Divinatory Arts: Tarot, Astrology, I Chin, Runes, Lithomancy, Radio esthesia, Interpretation of Dreams

2. Herbalism: amulets, incenses, oils, health, etc.

3. Healing Arts: Natural medicine, aromatherapy, psychic healing, crystals, Reiki, or other arts for healing

4. Arts with Relatives: Animal magic, Totems, changing forms, etc.

5. Talismans: creation of talismans and amulets.

6. Ritual Tools: creation of ritual tools

7. Psychic Arts: astral travel, telepathy, clairvoyance, psychometrics, etc.

8. Enchantment: Words of power, charms, spells, Songs and mantras

9. Fascination: Work in trance, Meditation, Hypnosis, Pathworking

10. Music: Music, tell stories, theater, etc.

More titles can be created according to Coven's need and with the approval of the advice.

Membership Status

The membership of any person can be withdrawn, suspended or terminated by Coven Council decision, either for lack of assistance, participation or for violation of the Wiccan Administration network and Operation.

The Coven Council

They are the maximum authority of Coven regarding its administration. Membership: The members of the council are all those who have been initiated. The Dedicators may be invited to participate in meetings.

Scope: The Council discusses and resolves issues related to: Activity program, Dedication, Initiations and Finance Memberships and budgets. Reach to the community: The High Priest or High Priestess, occupies the chair of presidency in the advice. When he is present, he will occupy that position immediately in the hierarchical rank.

Work Method: Decisions will be taken by consensus. In case of not reaching an agreement between the Initiates, the final decision will be taken by the Regent who will then consider what has been discussed, and will make a decision. Unless the Regent does not be the High Priest or the High Priestess, all decisions must be made in the same board meeting.

Meetings: The Council must meet at least once every three months, or under need on the part of some initiate. The necessary quorum must be at least three quarters of the Active initiates of Coven. Crafts and Jobs

High Priests (3rd Grade): President of the Coven Council, Coordination of Program of Studies, Counseling, Leadership in Rituals, Supervision of other officers, Directs initiations, Supervision of the work of candidates for the second and third degree. Coven representative, Maintain harmony in Coven, provides guidance tithe works of Coven, fight in defense of Coven when he is threatened, and it is the Final authority in regard to Ritual, Initiation, Ordination and everything related to religion.

Maiden (2nd Grade): Assists the High Priestess in her duties and assumes that role in absence of him. Sumoner (2nd Grade): Assists the High Priest in his duties and assumes that role in absence of it. Notify Coven members about meetings and other important information. Watchtower: Responsible for Coven Security, being responsible for planning of rituals, and special activities.

Write: Keeps the minutes of the Coven Council meetings, as well as the Coven property reports. Other functions can be created temporarily or permanently according to the Coven needs. All Dedicators and

Members must be guided in their conduct according to the Wiccan Network, the Law of Return, The Wiccan Laws, and the Gods within you.

Esbats will normally be held on full or new moon nights. Sabbats will be held on the corresponding day or on the weekend more close to the date, with the exception of Samhain to be performed on the night of 31 October. Once the dates for the rituals are marked, they cannot be changed unless more than two members cannot attend, for which a new date will be set again with the consensus of all Initiates.

Presentation seminars and open classes can be determined by the Coven Council as many times as necessary Classes for Dedicators and Initiates must be taught at least once a month on a date determined by the Coven Council. The Curriculum must be determined by the Coven Council. No amount will be set as payment for the dictated classes that are part of the Coven curriculum.

The New Moons are private esbats, only for devotees and Initiates. Full Moons are open to all those who want to participate. Sabbats can be opened, but in that case the Council must mark another date for celebration for members of Coven. The Coven Council or High Priests will determine if classes are open or closed. Dedicators and Initiates must participate in all Rituals and Classes for their level.

First Grade Dedicators and Initiates have compulsory attendance at least minus 75% of these activities, if this is not fulfilled your membership will be reviewed by the advice. The Second and Third Degree Initiates are Exempt from this obligation, given the level of work at Coven that is expected of them. Coven tickets are based on donations, or income from activities carried out in the community.

The Scribe must keep Coven's books raising reports for each meeting of the advice. Members addresses, phone numbers, and any other information related to particular individuals of Coven should be kept secret, and not discovering in front of people not belonging to Coven without the permission of the same.

Failure to member privacy is a serious offense and the penalty is termination of his membership, since it is considered as a breach of the Wiccan network. Any part of these laws may be amended or changed by the consensus of the Coven Council

THE WICCA SABBATS

There are eight Sabbats during the wiccan year. These are days to celebrate, rejoice with the gods and have a good time. No magic work is done in the Sabbats, unless it is a health work that is desperately necessary. But what does abound is joy and celebration. In ancient times, before the persecutions, many different covens gathered to celebrate. The number of sorcerers reached many hundreds, all from the covens scattered throughout the region.

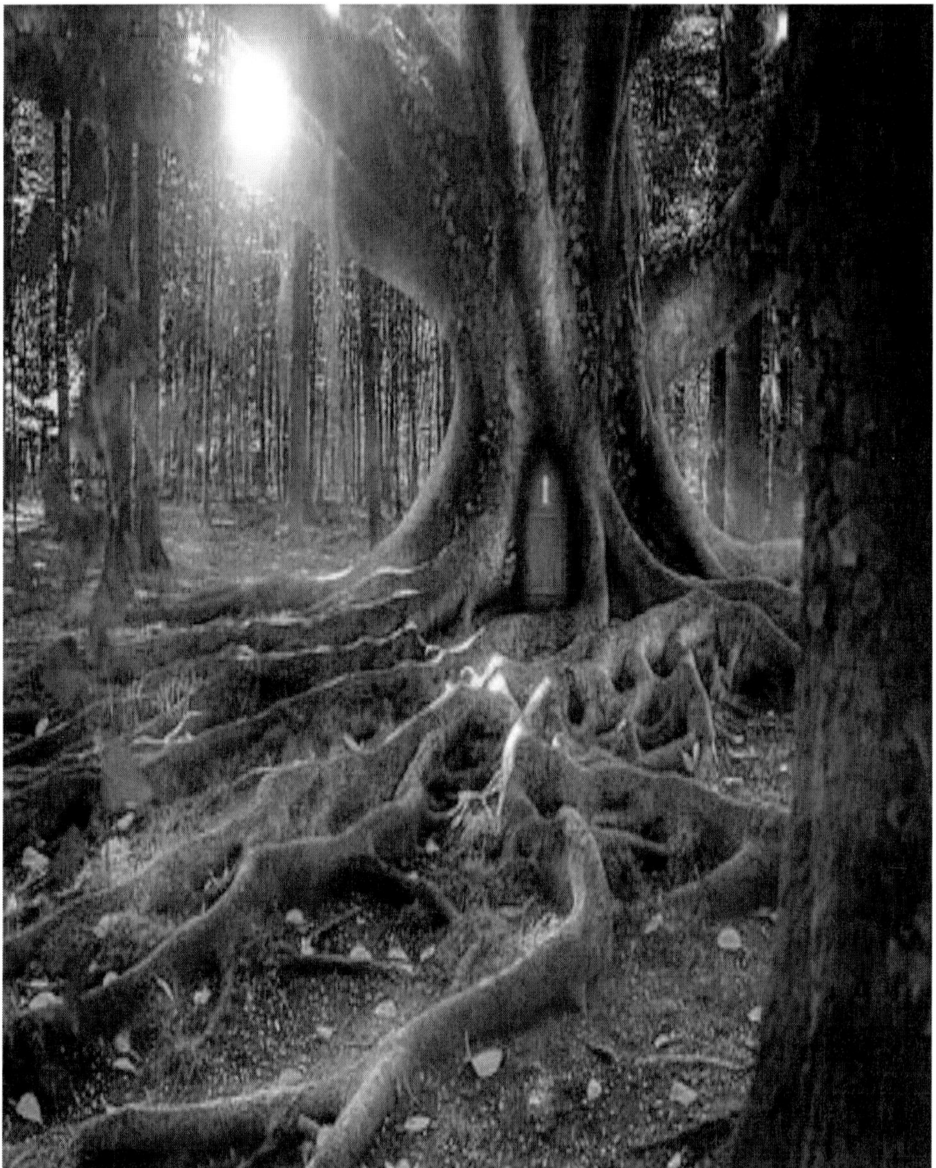

Chapter 2 – The Link Between Wicca And Witchcraft

The people in a group wooded hill on the shores of the Missouri River. Stars shine around the full moon above the surrounding trees. In between the old oaks, fireflies buzzing flashing their lights mysterious things. The night air is still, still. Forty people surround a burning bonfire, hands given, their attentions turned to a woman standing before from the bonfire. From her silhouetted silhouette against the glow of their das arises an invocation to the Goddess. The words, soft at first, growing stronger and stronger, clear well from your mouth. "Moon goddess," she says, "every year we gather here tonight on a full moon in your name."Sticks crackle in the fire."God of the Sun, O Magnificent, almighty ...".The invocation comes to an end. The woman raises her arms to the heavens as the group begins to move towards lime at a slow pace. The people - come dressed in with hoods, some with mundane clothes -They took their steps. They sing in a slow single tone, the impossible principle to understand. The wood crackles. The moonlight spills out.

Bare feet tap in the floor. Fast. The group practically flies around the go and the woman standing between them as they return their minds for their purpose. After an immeasurable time, the lonely woman just stops them. The group stops instantly, and their members at the same time they point their hands at the figure. It shines, radiates, shakes, and directs energy through the projected to the Goddess represented by the glowing sphere in heaven. Exhausted, the group sits on the bare earth. Observed burning the fire, they talk and laugh and share wine and cakes in the form of crescents. Your rite is finished. Popular magic is only part of what is commonly called the sea of witchcraft.

The other part is represented by religion known as Wicca. There are at least five main elements which distinguish Wicca from other religions, which are: Goddess and God worship; Reverence for the earth; Acceptance of magic; Acceptance of Reincarnation; Absence of Proselytism. Wiccans worship Goddess and God. Western religion current dental care, according to the Wiccans, is unbalanced. Waistband-it is called the Godhead Deity (instead of Goddess). God the Father is a common term. The concept of "saviors" but culminates, direct descendants of the male Deities, is both found, even outside Christianity. The re-representatives of these organizations - officers, priests and I do more harm than good. They fight against strips that cut down trees and cover acres of land with concrete and tar. For seeing the earth as a manifestation Goddess and God, the Wiccans care about their well-being: they lend the earth human energy so that recover from the damage inflicted on her by humanity. Therefore, Wicca is really a religion of the Earth.

Magic, as we have seen, plays a role in almost all religions. At Wicca, she has a more prominent role you. Wicca is not religious magic, despite its following. Pains certainly to practice. Nor is it religion magic. It is a religion that encompasses magic, received viewing it as an opportunity to tune into the divine, earthly and human energies. Because Wicca is a true religion, magic has a secondary role in their rituals. Even in a practical rite aimed at a specific magical end, the Goddess and the God are always invoked before the energy is sent. The magical aspects of Wicca confuse the laity, perhaps because in most other religions it is believed that only priests or saviors can in one mine, channel the divine energy. Wicca is not so exclusive; she sees magic as a natural part of life and of religion. Reincarnation is an ancient teaching that most The Wiccan tradition sees it as reality. Basically, the riper-Carnation is the doctrine of rebirth - the phenomenon of incarnation in the human form, aiming at the evolution of soul without sex or age. While reincarnation is not an external concept, including Wicca, she is happily accepted by most Wiccans for providing answers to many questions about the everyday life and for offering explanations for phenomena more mystical as death, birth, and karma. Some may say, "Reincarnation? Bah! That just is a thing of the East. "Undoubtedly, more is known about their incarnation through the teachings from the region today known as India. However, the idea itself is pro-as old as humanity itself. A seed falls into the soil. It germinates and flourishes. They unfold. The sprouts lengthen and explode in flower. The seeds fall into the soil. The plant withers and withers but next spring another plant will emerge from the soil. The doctrine of reincarnation may have originated from the conservation of natural processes like this one. Those who accept its reality, including many Wiccans, They gave it comforting.

The fifth biggest difference between Wicca and most other religions is the absence of proselytizing. Nobody went; yahoo will be pressed to become a Wiccano. Not there are threats of eternal fire and damnation, or punishment for do not practice Wicca. Goddess and God are not Deities jealous and the Wiccans do not fear them or are under-jugados. Initiation candidates (which we will talk about more in throughout this book) do not condemn their old faiths. Wicca doesn't it's a brainwashing and human-control cult disguised as religion. Wiccans do not recruit new supporters while they harelips and rub their hands as the people enter their religion. There are no missionaries from Wicca, or "witnesses", or pressure groups. It may be surprising to those educated according to the mentality of orthodox religions but Wicca is based on a safe and solid concept that is the antithesis of the teach-most other religions: no religion imperfect for all. Perhaps it is no exaggeration to say that the greatest form of human vanity is to assume that their religion is the only Deity and that all will judge it so highly recommended thinker like you, and those with different beliefs they are deceived, deluded or ignorant. It is understandable that many religions and their followers think this way and take part in the conversion. Watching others convert to their restored faith clarifies its genuineness in the mind of the converter. Some members of orthodox religions are really concerned with the souls of unbelievers, but this is based on the dull teachings of their religions. Another aspect of proselytizing involves politics. If Religion A converts Country B, it increases its political power and financial in that country. The same is true of people as well. Orthodox religions have unlimited influence at the governmental and financial level. Political candidates sponsored by the major religions are constantly elected to then propose or support legislation that would broaden the interests of that religion. This can all happen. To undermine (voters may ignore the real nature or extent of the applicant's links with the organized religion), but the effects are the same. Money is also a powerful incentive forth word is propagated.

Today, the religions established in The United States makes monthly billions of dollars from taxes. Right, a portion of this money is for of charity but the bulk of it goes to the bureaucracy of that religion, fattening the bank accounts of the individuals who control it. So the more followers, the more money. Wicca just isn't like that. It is not organized to this point. There are national groups but for the most part you for social and sometimes legal reasons. Regional Meetings Wiccans can attract hundreds of people, but local people usually have less than ten members, and many Wiccans practice their religion alone, without affiliation. To some group, Wicca is not a financial institution and does not struggle to become one. Students do not pay to be initiated. Small fees, if any, resemble charges by various groups to cover food expenses, drinks and so on. Pertaining to a world organization that wants to control the world is untrue. As are the lies about Wiccans who try to coerce others into adhering to their religion. They simply are not so insecure. Don't worry, the Wiccans aren't wandering around trying to force young Jimmy into a convenor persuade Aunt Sara to give up her savings. They are pleased with the practice of their religion to their own way - either alone or with others. They are differences between Wicca and other religions as well as as the ultimate goal of all: union with the Divine.

Although it was written for a solitary practitioner, most was created for group work, even if only one individual is involved in creating the circle. It never hurts to repeat that the "Stone Spirits" above are not disembodied human souls - they are not spirits, demons or capitals. They are what some Wiccan traditions often call "Lord of the Tor-Watchers "or" Queens and Kings of the Elements."These are elemental energies that are invited to attend the protection as well as to share your energy special philosophy. This practice is almost universal in Wicca. According to Wiccano's idea, the circle is considered as the holiest place to honor the Goddess and God, but it also has a second function: contain and concentrate magic energy. This is a secondary function. Certainly, the circle is not necessary for the effective practice of group or solitary magic. Basically, the magic circle is a non-physical temple, but real, in which humans - Wiccans - walk along Goddess and God. As such, it is one of the main characteristics of Wicca practice, but it is not at all needed for group worship.

Wiccans can practice simple rituals while walking alone on hills, or sit on the beach, watching the water. They can commune with the Goddess and with God as the sun rises or the moon disappears. A Wiccan group can during a picnic or a stroll inland, suddenly decide to practice some kind of ritual. Without instruments, they can simply sit or stand in a circle and practice your work. During all rituals other than spontaneous, however, the magic circle is usually built, and is within it is the sphere of energy that the rites of worship and magic are practiced. The circle (sphere) of energy is the temple of Wicca.

Chapter 3 – Learning Wiccan Spells

There are many forms of magic and folk magic is nothing but a form of them. The two other major types - *ceremonial* and *religious* - do not fit our definition of Witchcraft because they are usually grouped together with all other hidden practices under this title, a brief discussion on they can clear up some misunderstandings.

Ceremonial Magic

Ceremonial (or ritual) magic is a contemporary system based on ancient and relatively ancient traditions. It is based on Sumerian, Egyptian, Indian, and Semitic magic, influenced by Arab thought and subsequently So. Freemasonry also contributed to its current structure, as well as the secret societies so popular in Britain and throughout Europe in the 18th and 19th centuries. Contrary to popular opinion, wizard's ceremonials have nothing to do with the demolition of or the theft of magic rings of monstrous spirits with fly heads. They do not have magic rugs or live in caves, and certainly do not jam swords into victims' bodies do not even have goblins as money. Most importantly, they have no connection with Witchcraft, except in the minds of the laity.

The ritual structures, terminology, and objectives of the Ceremonial magicians are usually - but not always -in union with the divine, with perfection and expansion of consciousness. Or, as commonly described, "science and the conversation with a wizard's guardian angel."A grand spiritual goal, no? And indicates one of the basic differences between ceremonial magic and pop up home. Unlike the latter, ritual mages usually don't care about the goals of the popular wizard: love, healing, money, happiness, and protection. When such goals are accessed through ceremonial magic (as in the creation of a talisman), is usually like the means to an end - achieve the above union. For their part, wizards solve problems in their lives with rituals and rare mind seek something beyond. Some ceremonial wizards organize themselves into groups known as stores or orders (like the famous Golden Dawn - Golden Dawn, no. of T.), and use elements of the Egyptian religion when creating their magical works. Many of rituals used by a small group of this magic shop from the late last century were published in The Golden Dawn, by Israel Regardie, one of the most influential ma-already edited. Other wizards tune into more orthodox religions.xas. The magical books of the Middle Ages and Renaissance included invocations to Jehovah, Adonai, and God, and use extensive Judeo-Christian terminology. This is not heresy or farce, but the product of a different interpretation of the Christian myth. Of course, this is nothing like folk magic in which power is sent without the invocation of a Deity. Ceremonial wizards tend to be somewhat individual lists. Many practice their art alone, dedicating long evenings reading ancient scriptures, preparing their "instruments of art "and learning Latin and Greek to better practice their rituals. They study the works of Aleister Crowley, as well as those of William Gray, John Dee, Franz Bardon, Agrippa, Dion For-tune and many other authors. Some dive into alchemy, geomancy, Enochian magic, and other subjects such as main or secondary aspects of their studies. Ceremonial wizards are simply human beings who not only work with energy (that is, they practice ma-also seek something bigger that they were not able to find in orthodox religions. They have a long colorful story behind them, full of fantastic events and exotic rituals and rites. But they are not Wizards.

Herbs

Possibly, the eivas were first used magic and religion long before they were thrown in pans for culinary or medicinal purposes. Currently, were rediscovered by new generations of powerful wizards were jumping, busy harvesting, mixing, cooking and preparing these aromatic treasures. Herbs, like crystals, have very strong energies specific and distinct, which are used in magic. Petals of roses can be scattered around the house to provide peace. They can also be placed between candles pink to bring love to the life of the popular wizard. A CA-it can be burned to stimulate intelligence; the flowers lavender can be added to the bath for purifiers, and the sandalwood burned to raise the ion and mediumistic experiences. An incredible variety of herbs - including fruits, trees, flowers, roots, chestnuts, seeds, algae, ferns, grass and all other types of plant material - is used in folk magic. This is a form of magic that is not we completely forgot because we still offer flowers, dear people, we use perfumes and essences vegetables to attract mates, we serve meals enhanced with herbs for potential lovers (or we received them). Eivas can be burned as incense to release energies in the air, or carried in their pockets and sprinkled around the house for various magic purposes. Oils essentials and magical mixtures are rubbed into the body or candles, added to the bath or used to anoint crystals and other objects in ritual preparations. Once the domain of every healer and wizard, the herbs once again they are used as instruments of power by many popular mages.

Chapter 4 - Wicca Terminologies

This chapter is intended to be a small summary of the terms most used by sorcerers and witches, to serve as an approach to the subject and then allow the analysis of deeper and more advanced topics:

BRUJERIA: is the use of magical techniques to act on nature, acts through symbolic principles, through more or less explicit, violent and bloody, not only to seek benefit, but seeks to do evil and generally gets a monetary payment in return. Although religion and high magic denigrate witchcraft, there are many macho prejudices about women who come from the church and witchcraft in many cases it was a spiritual technique that sought the union of the soul with nature through the forces of the elements, that aspect is being rescued by the wiccans.

FACING: is the use of magic to obtain benefits, to achieve advantages and satisfying the ego implies the use of intelligence to turn the cosmic laws in our favor. Although they are not bloody and violent like witchcraft, implies a poisoning of the soul and mind twists and becomes cynical, uses the same laws of magic, but controlled by the ego, in sorcerers are called black magicians.

WICCA: it is an old and Nordic term, it is the root of Withcraft. Nowadays Wicca is a cultural movement that seeks to review and repair the injustice of history with witches and rescue their rituals from a spiritual perspective, as a union of the soul with nature and hopefully witchcraft let it go seen wrong and managed to be understood by the globalized culture, because if the wicca fights against their own negative aspects and celebrates and invokes the positive natural forces in the experience of self-discovery of the soul.

MAGIC: It is the art and practice of working with nature and its forces and producing modifications, usually divided into various types of magic and its 2 main branches are Goercia and Teurgia. Magic is usually divided into natural, which is done with potions and objects, in spells that are made with the voice, the gestural magic that uses magnetic passes and the etheric energy and magic work by thought, the most powerful.

GOERCIA: It is the magic applied to the demons and inferior spirits. It is the classic practice that is taught in magical manuals or grimoires like little Alberto or the book of almaziel or the salomonicos.

THEURGY: The part of magic applied to the spiritual, to the bright forces, involves the invocation and work with angels and entities, includes the mental magic and karmic transmutatory processes, their rituals are those of the great religions and divine and angelic invocations.

NIGROMANCE: the part of magic and sorcery that deals primarily with the evocation of the dead, of obtaining clairvoyance through them or messages through the dead, as well as ceremonies of invocation of the dead and works of magic that they involve spirits and energies of already deceased people. It is the most repudiated part of magic, however its action on matter and nature is powerful. Today there are few shamans who practice it and most powerful necromancers are the Vodu and Santero priests of Central America.

AQUELARRE: It is also called sabbat (sabath). It is the meeting of the witches, it began with the narration of the misdeeds of each one and continued with a banquet (with great delicacies or truculent characters according to the versions) and culminated with a great orgy.

COVENS: The mountains of Blockberg and Koterberg in Germany, the plain of Barabona, in Soria (Spain), are places where it is said covens were celebrated. Much of what is said about covens are versions that the church extracted as a confession with torture, much of what is said is symbolic andesoteric and not literal and much of what the witches said to do, like flying on brooms and their unions with beastly beings, were the product of hallucinogenic mixtures that have been found and reproduced containing belladonna, poppy, mandragora and other hallucinogenic products that generate the same type of hallucination with beings, which produces LSD in the hippies of the 60s. Most coven phenomena, visions and rituals are made in the astral plane and they are internal experiences of the astral bass in low and lugubrious regions.

GRIMORIO: The witches kept a diary in which they cast their spells and studied their effects, so they were transmitted and enduring. The most famous is the

BOOK OF SHADOWS, ridiculed by mediocre TV series, but the book exists and is a collection of basic and traditional rituals, which includes several volumes; the most famous grimoires are mentioned in the middle ages, when the uglesia prohibits books other than the bible and grimoires become almost science books and of instruction. Also, most grimoires have recipes with ingredients impossible to achieve and doubtful results. They also exaggerate in the magic of invocaion of spirits and submit to the intake and proof of all Menjunjes and prepared class, but in all of them there is a good base with recipes, practices and some rituals and a lot of mental preparation and suggestion to produce the effects on its surroundings, but some recipes do work and it is not only a suggestion. The most famous grimoires are the various clavicles of Salomon, the book of raziel, the books by john dee with enoquiana magic (angelica), the agrippa treaties are the most complete manuals, the books of arbatel and abremalin the magician, the grimoireslate as the little and the great alberto, the book of cipriano, pactum and several hundred more, some with more value than others. They are difficult to obtain and demand a serious study, because their recipes usually hide esoteric and symbolic descriptions before real or physical processes.

CONJURO: Formulas that fulfilled the function of reinforcing spells, in general spells were formulas with words that mixed ancient languages with strange rhymes, and they were basically a vibratory projection, through which desire it manifested itself through the word and produced a projection in the etheric planes which then rushed and manifested on the physical plane over others. Spells are complicated and are already formulas for the evocation of entities, the grimoires usually include some magic recipes and some more spells or disguised children.

FACT: it is a manipulation of the appearance, based on the manipulation of ether fluids, over the etheric body and the aura. The spells changed the appearance of things or the mood of people, were manipulation of etheric energy or of astral substance and are already typical magical operations.

CHARMING: it is a spell that is cast on a place, parapsychology called as an infestation, when a place seems to accumulate and manifest energies conflicting and phenomenal called poltergeist for science today, enchantment is a mantle of generally oppressive energy that is projected and confined to a place and that energy encloses entities present there and affects them, having these that manifest the enchantments are similar to the evocations and manipulations that are made with spirits, but these are made with energy, because the municipalities are the same.

FILTER: preparation consisting of liquids that also involve handling of subtle fluids, to impress and affect people's minds and emotions, are classic filters used to divert enemies, to fall in love and to manipulate psychologically then with witchcraft rituals. In general the filter can serve as it helps up to a point where it becomes something bad and a means of doing evil, which is usually harmful for the subject that ends up losing or ruining that with the filter intended. Since the filter is basically an illusion, which can be used as an opportunity, but its duration is fleeting and is usually ruined and decomposed like this.

EIGHTH OR POTION: prepared generally based on liquids, which included drugs and substances that manifested the analogical properties or correspondences that thematic attributed to objects, minerals, vegetables, animals and emotional forces that related and reflected the planetary and angelic forces, in turn reflecting the cosmic forces and divine attributes.

MEJUNJE OR MENJUNGE: preparation of narcotic herbs that it provided to witches the sensation of flying, by extension any herbal preparation that produces some effect on nature such as extraordinary cures, divination or discharge of negative energies.

INCUBO: the devil in the form of a man, so women used to present themselves to seduce her and turn them into witches.

SUCUBO: the devil in the form of a woman, his malefic function was to seduce the men: most of the primitive saints suffered temptations on the part of sucubos.

ENGENDROS: The beings products of the union of humans and diabolic beings as sucubos and incubations, contrary to the general opinion, there are several chronicles births of these fabulous beings, who manifested a strange appearance and even more strange phenomena surrounded them.

HOMUNCLE, HOMOID OR ANDROID: an artificially produced creature, in the cabin is the golem made of clay, in the voodoo are the resurrected zombies, the homunculi are creatures produced in laboratories of the alchemists that gave rise to legends like Frankenstein's, Androids are creatures animated by magical or mechanical procedures, celebrate the android that destroyed shots of aquino, the homunculus of paracels, some creatures that were produced and the wanderings of the golem in prague at the beginning century, fighting against the Nazis.

DAIMON: family spirit or guardian who carries the person and advises and inspires, according to the Greek tradition and is cited by Plato and Pythagoras, it is confused with other beliefs as the holy guardian angel and the djinns or Persian geniuses, although it seems to be a metaphor of consciousness and its mysterious voice.

METAMORPHOSIS: belief that humans can transform into animals (preferably wolves) through concoctions and special rites. In general the transformation is related to the moon, because when going out at night it symbolizes the repressed subconscious forces that come out and manifest themselves, thus the transformation is the expression of the aura or ethereal body that manifests an animistic trait. The transformation into wolves or vampires is the most common, it was said that witches are turned into cats or toads and with respect to the transformation itself, it seems to be a transformation of the ethereal body, the aura, which manifests in the form the features. This process has been documented in the mediums that have materialized ectoplasm, a materialization of ethereal substance and the process would be similar.

BLACK MASS: parody of the Christian mass that the devil does in the covens and that it ended with the blasphemous kiss on the butt of the officiates although it is not known, the ritual elements of the Catholic mass are Babylonians and the Mass Black is a celebration of nature and the inferior and powerful aspects of instinct.

DEMONIC: the demonic is a journey down to the bottom, to the instinct and the power, violence and chaos, just as the opposite is meditation, a journey of ascent towards the regions of light or knowledge.

Conclusion

Thank you for making it through to the end of *Wicca For Beginners*, let's hope it was informative and able to provide you with all of the tools you need to achieve your goals whatever they may be.

The time has come to get rid of our preconceived notions and analyze the purposes of Witchcraft: conquest spiritual and happy and financially secure existence. Where is the horror of this? Where are the horrors that zillions of sermons and that even today contribute for religious crimes?

Horror exists only in the minds of those unknown to the truth, and this lack of knowledge breeds fear. Such fear is fuelled by representatives of other religions who use it to increase their adhesions.

Popular magic and Wicca are gentle and love, practiced by hundreds of thousands of people sounds. That is the truth about Witchcraft today.

Finally, if you found this book useful in any way, a review on Amazon is always appreciated!

Made in United States
North Haven, CT
21 October 2022